History for their Masters

History for their Masters

OPINION IN THE ENGLISH HISTORY TEXTBOOK:
1800–1914

by VALERIE E. CHANCELLOR

with a foreword by Sir John Newsom

---

*I believe it will be absolutely necessary that you
should prevail on our future masters to learn their
letters.*

(Speech by Robert Lowe in the House of Commons
on the passing of the Reform Bill, 1867, and popularly
remembered as 'We must educate our masters.')

ADAMS & DART

First published in 1970 by
Adams & Dart, 40 Gay Street, Bath, Somerset
SBN 239 00068 4

Printed in Great Britain by
Alden & Mowbray Ltd
at the Alden Press, Oxford

Foreword

The study of opinions and ideas in children's literature is an important, but until recently neglected, branch of educational research. It is partly by historical surveys of the traditions of society as passed on to the young that we may judge how these traditions came to be selected and the extent of their effect upon the national consciousness. In particular we ought to consider how far they impede or promote necessary change within society in general and an educational system in particular.

It is my hope that Miss Chancellor's work will encourage and illuminate investigations into books used in schools today. Certainly there is need to consider how far they affect attitudes not only to international affairs but to problems of race, politics and religion at home. The past twenty years have shown an awareness that traditional concepts in these fields are not, necessarily, infallible. There is room here, as elsewhere, for re-appraisal.

Sir John Newsom CBE, LLD

Contents

ACKNOWLEDGEMENTS

I should like to thank the authorities of Birmingham University for permission to quote from the thesis on which this work is based. In particular, I must record my gratitude to Mrs Stella Jull of the Department of Education. It was she who first drew my attention to the present field of enquiry and by her patient and tactful guidance enabled my research to proceed.

Censorship and Selection

'What historian ever brought his reader to the scene
of an action and related the event circumstantially as
it happened ?'[1]

CONCERN at the sort of opinions expressed in history books for schools
is nothing new. The starting point of this study was the realisation
that the English educationalists of the last century were perhaps
more concerned than those of today to eliminate from textbooks, attitudes
which they considered harmful. Sometimes this concern was expended on
the obvious dangers of religious or political subversion; sometimes on
contentious questions of morality or nationalism. Only one major group
of opinions which might engage the attention of the modern reader went
almost unnoticed. In the days before Marxist ideas were generally familiar,
references to social class were not apparently regarded as controversial or
liable to give offence.

Contemporary comments on bias in the nineteenth-century history
textbook raise the whole question of how far there really was any systematic
censorship in the past. Of course, commercial considerations must have
governed how far any book was acceptable and militated against the
expression of extreme opinions unpalatable to the society of the time.
Textbooks have to be adjusted to the demands of the market. Apart from
this, however, there does arise the doubt as to whether a more conscious
and directed effort was made to indoctrinate the young with ideas acceptable to the dominant classes of society. Expressions of the desire to do so
abound. Robert Lowe's dictum about the need to 'educate our masters' is
among the best known of mis-quotations.[2] Even the more liberal and
enlightened W. E. Forster defended the Education Bill of 1870 on the
grounds that 'now we have given them political power we must not wait
any longer to give them education. There are questions demanding answers

---

[1] *On Education,* by G. Nicholson (1812), p. 342.
[2] For the exact source of this quotation, see title page.

[7]

which ignorant constituencies are ill-fitted to solve.'[1] Such remarks have given rise to suspicions that the growth of the state system of education in England was closely connected with the desire to mould working-class opinions into non-revolutionary and 'respectable' patterns which would leave the upper classes free to govern and to maintain their position in society in a supposedly democratic era.

Of all school subjects, history is perhaps the most obviously a vehicle for the opinions of the teacher and of the section of society which he represents. It gives scope for the expression of a wide variety of political, moral and religious ideas, and since these are embedded in a traditional and often emotive story, they are arguably more open to acceptance and less liable to detection by the pupil. These opinions readily form part of the patterns of thought which develop in the individual child as well as in society as a whole.[2] English society of the period 1800–1914, which witnessed the coming of popular education and of mass literacy, provides a special opportunity for the study of how ideas are passed on to the rising generation, how these ideas are selected and what relation, if any, they bear to those current in contemporary society as a whole. By examining the various opinions expressed in history textbooks of the period we might hope to examine one strand in this process and in particular one where we know that severe outside pressures were at work. The aim of this study is, therefore, not only to examine how far there really was any attempt to use the history textbook to mould the opinions of a future electorate in a growingly democratic age, but also to illuminate the way in which traditional wisdom is passed on to the rising generation.

It is as well to realise, however, that contemporaries were concerned with the problem of bias in history textbooks before the passing of the 1832 Reform Act which opened the way for the universal franchise in England. From the earliest years of the nineteenth century comments about the religious, moral and political attitudes to be found in history books which children might read are not uncommon. Writing in the *Guardian of Education*, Mrs Sarah Trimmer criticised the *Chronicle of the Kings of England* by Robert Dodsley on the grounds that: 'It was evidently composed with the most prophane and invidious design, to depreciate the sacred writings and to bring contempt and ridicule upon the memory of the

---

[1] Debate on the Education Bill (1870), p. 18.
[2] For reference to this, see also *The Developmental Psychology of Jean Piaget,* by J. H. Flavell. pp. 255–7.

sovereigns who have successively filled the British throne, and through them to glance derision upon the monarchy itself.'[1] In contrast, a writer in the same journal was drawn to praise 'a short narrative of the wonderful and providential preservation of King Charles II', since 'Tracts, expressly designed, as this is, to excite in the minds of children a spirit of loyalty to the king and attachment to the monarchical form of government are especially suited to the youth of Great Britain'.[2] Later an anonymous reviewer in the *Quarterly Journal of Education* declared that there was 'only one thing more in need of reform than school-masters and that is school-books'.[3] He went on to commend *Stories from English History*, by Mrs Hack. Its achievement was to 'impart correct historical knowledge and at the same time to convey beautiful lessons of morality, the highest and best use of history'. It was also praised for its 'entire freedom from all party spirit and bias'.

Of all historians whose work was sometimes used by children, Hume seems to have caused the most disquiet. Hannah More numbered him among the 'infidel historians'.[4] While admitting his attractive style of writing, she damned his history as 'a serpent under a bed of roses'. Especially serious was his tolerant scepticism with regard to religion which might lead the young reader to assume that 'the Reformation was not really worth contending for'.[5] Moreover, Hume's history could never be trusted even where it appeared unbiased because . . . 'he has shown his principle so fully in some of his other works that we are entitled to read with suspicion everything he says on the borders of religion'.[6] Elsewhere Hume was castigated as 'the avowed enemy of the two principles which conduce most to the happiness of mankind; religion and liberty; and he who makes him the standard of his historic faith, will embrace innumerable errors, arising not merely from design but from negligence'.[7]

As state intervention in education tended to increase throughout the nineteenth century, the problem of bias in history textbooks for schools became more acute. The anonymous writer of an article in the Congregationalist journal, *The Educator*, remarked that a recent Bill raised the

---

[1] *Guardian of Education* (1802), p. 68.
[2] Ibid. Sept. 1806, vol. V, pp. 422–3.
[3] *Quarterly Journal of Education* (1831), p. 220.
[4] More's *Hints* (1805), p. 155.
[5] Ibid. p. 157.
[6] Ibid. p. 160.
[7] *On Education*, by G. Nicholson (1812), p. 345.

question of the teaching of history in secular schools, and went on to express his fears that the religious implications of the subject would lead to a watered-down version of the facts being presented to avoid giving offence to Roman Catholics.[1] However, those who wanted state schools were undeterred by this and other sectarian arguments. By the 1870 Education Act these were to be set up by newly elected School Boards to supplement the efforts of voluntary societies. The Boards were soon drawn to consider the selection and censorship of history textbooks.

Writing on the teaching of history in the *School Board Chronicle*, John Baker Hopkins put forward the view that: 'In history only names and dates are trustworthy and the former are frequently corrupted and the latter are generally wrong.' He went on to stress the importance of teaching history in shaping young minds. 'Very few men forsake the religious creed they are taught in childhood; and it is not less usual for men to cleave to the political creed they learn from histories.'[2] In the same issue of the *School Board Chronicle* appeared an account of a discussion taken from the *London School Board Chronicle* for 30 March 1872, as to whether control or censorship of textbooks was in fact justified.[3] In a notable plea for freedom, the Rev. J. A. Picton declared: 'Our main safeguard against a revolution was the patriotic love of one's country arising from a knowledge of the past, leading men to see how much preferable a gradual reform was to violent changes. . . . He belonged to a certain denomination which boasted a glorious history, but their progenitors committed many grievous mistakes which he should not like to see repeated. He would rather place in the hands of a child a book which did some wrong to the different denominations than he would keep it altogether ignorant of its country's history. Picton then went on to argue: 'The children who attend our elementary schools are not parrots, but reasonable beings, and they are able to judge a tree by its fruit.' It is interesting to note that he here stresses patriotism and opposition to revolution as desirable attitudes which should be found in history books, though he was enlightened enough to oppose not only censorship but also excessive moralising. 'Facts and not judgments' were what Picton looked for in a good history textbook.

Not surprisingly in view of the sectarian controversies which preceded

---

[1] *The Educator* (1852), vol. II, p. 44. Reprinted from the *Scottish Education and Literary Journal.*
[2] *School Board Chronicle* (13 April 1872), p. 279.
[3] Ibid. p. 279.

the 1870 Education Act, it was apparently the religious aspect of history teaching which worried school boards the most. The *School Board Chronicle* reported a difference of opinion among the members of the Birmingham School Board over the purchase of *Nelson's Reading Books* for the boys' school of the People's Chapel, Great King Street, and the infants' school at the Wesleyan Chapel in Unett Street.[1] The Rev. Canon O'Sullivan objected to the new books because of their obviously protestant bias. He took particular exception to the sentence: 'They were Tyndale's Testaments, ferreted out by emissaries of the Cardinal, who had swept every cranny in search of the hated thing.' O'Sullivan argued that no Cardinal would refer to the Bible as a 'hated thing'. However, he did not take his opposition to the point of voting against the purchase of the readers as Joseph Chamberlain and other members of the Board did. In an editorial in the same issue the *School Board Chronicle* was also able to report that a dissenting member of the Birmingham School Board had opposed the purchase of a book on the grounds that a passage in it was found to imply the truth of the doctrine of the Trinity.[2] At the same time the London School Board had been unable to recommend an English history class book on the grounds that its religious bias was suspect. The *School Board Chronicle* came out firmly against censorship. Children, it claimed, 'should be taught boldly and with as few restrictions as possible'. It further suggested that only laymen should be elected to School Boards, presumably on the grounds that they would be less likely to censor books for religious reasons than the clergy. After these initial attempts on the part of School Boards to control the contents of history textbooks, the matter was apparently dropped. The *Educational Times* for July 1873 mentions that they had recently found the difficulty of selecting impartial history text-books so great that 'they decided to adopt the oral system of teaching, preferring to leave the matter in the hands of the master to adopting any of the existing objectionable textbooks on the subject'.[3]

Of course, other factors besides the criticism of reviewers and those with control over the purchase of school books governed the selection of material by authors and thus incidentally the attitudes displayed in their work. The influence of leading academic and literary historians on history textbooks used by children must, for instance, have been considerable. Some of the

---

[1] *School Board Chronicle* (1 March 1873), p. 56.
[2] *School Board Chronicle* (1 March 1873), p. 66.
[3] *Educational Times* (1 July 1873), p. 88.

latter contain passages which were lifted verbatim from histories intended for the adult market. Few of them made any claim to be works of original scholarship and even where the author rewrote his source of information in his own words, he must have absorbed the judgments which it contained. Thus the greater stress on the idea of progress and the widespread adoption of what has become known as the 'Whig Interpretation' of history in many textbooks during the nineteenth century may be partly linked with the influence of Hallam and Macaulay. Likewise Carlyle's well-known dictum that 'the History of the World is but the biography of great men'[1] is possibly reflected to some extent in the tendency, especially among writers of the historical reader, to recount history as a series of stories about great men and women. The influence of Stubbs and Maitland is often to be seen in the increased attention to constitutional history in works for senior pupils towards the latter part of the nineteenth century. At the same time the growth of the new 'scientific' school of historians led by J. B. Bury and others was no doubt largely responsible for the increased accuracy and sobriety of expression to be found in some of the textbooks written by reputable academic historians who shunned the dramatic and literary qualities of those who preferred to follow in the way of Macaulay. The work of J. R. Green contributes another notable influence on the development of textbooks in the later nineteenth century. Several editions of his great work *A Short History of the English People* were prepared for schools after 1874 when it appeared for the first time,[2] and it was undoubtedly in part responsible for the increasing emphasis on social history to be found in some textbooks.

The influence of fashions in literature and other forms of cultural activity is also apparent in the school books of the period. The revival of interest in the Middle Ages which showed itself in the Gothic style of architecture and furnishings as well as in painting and literature throughout the nineteenth century is generally reflected in the great importance assigned to the medieval period in history textbooks of that date. Figures such as Richard Whittington and the Little Princes in the Tower are often dealt with at a length surprising to the modern reader. Connected with the Gothic revival, the Romantic movement generally seems to have been responsible for the idealisation of such 'romantic figures' as Mary, Queen

---

[1] *Heroes and Hero Worship*, by T. Carlyle (1908 ed.), p. 239
[2] For example, C. W. A. Tait's *Analysis of English History* (1878) was based on Green's work.

of Scots, who is sympathetically treated on the whole, although her conduct and views violated the deepest moral and religious principles of
Victorian England.[1] The influence of the romantic movement on textbooks
can also be seen in the choice of illustrations, many of which must appear
extremely sentimental to modern eyes.

Another factor governing the selection of material in school books is,
of course, the methods of teaching in vogue at the time. At the end of the
eighteenth century children tended to be regarded as adults in miniature
who must, therefore, be content with cut-down rather than simplified
versions of histories intended for adult readers—hence Mrs Trimmer's fear
that Dodsley's history would be used in the school room.[2] However, they
were expected to memorise a store of facts which apparently had to be
repeated parrot fashion. The popularity of Miss Magnall's questions on
history which were repeatedly reissued until late in the nineteenth century
reflects this. So does the number of mnemonic histories which set out to
help the pupils memorise a series of arbitrarily chosen and barely related
facts. For instance, W. Frank Matthews of the Townsend School, Kidder-
minster, developed a system by which letters of the alphabet were paired
and given a corresponding number, e.g. B & M = 1, C & N = 2. Vowels
counted as zero. In the history itself the capital letters at the beginning
of words in each line indicated the date at which the event occurred:

1	5	0	9

Book against Reformation, Excommunication and Vegetable.

1	5	1	7

Martin the Reformer Began his Task.

1	5	1	8

Magellan the Rover round America Went.[3]

However, even at the beginning of the nineteenth century there was a
movement against excessive memorising of meaningless historical facts.
In the preface to history, Edward Baldwin wrote of his readers: 'Too long
have their tender memories been overloaded with a variety of minute
particulars, which as they excite no passion in the mind, and present no
picture, can be learned only to be forgotten.'[4] Later Baldwin's view became
almost universally accepted, if Knight, another author, is to be believed.

---

[1] See later pp. 83–4.
[2] See above p. 8–9.
[3] Matthews (*c.*1840), p. 6.
[4] Baldwin (1812), preface p. iii.

[13]

He wrote that 'school instruction in History has ceased to mean the learning by rote of the dates of prominent events, which fade from the memory in the absence of all interesting associations'.[1] Even writers of high academic distinction were prepared to adapt their material to the needs of their child readers. For instance, F. C. J. Hearnshaw, Professor of History at King's College, London, claimed that his work was adapted to the earlier stages of a child's development and was meant to stimulate interest in history while remaining scholarly and accurate in approach.[2] Where history textbooks became much more than lists of facts to be memorised, the opinions of the authors were more frequently expressed and assumed greater importance.

In order to discover something of the exact nature of these opinions and their relation to those commonly held elsewhere at the time, it was necessary to select and classify them according to various general groups. These are based on aspects of bias which contemporary reviewers most frequently remarked upon, namely political, moral, religious and nationalistic. The only addition is a group to include opinions on social class. In view of accusations of indoctrination in the state educational system it was necessary to examine the social backgrounds of authors in order to gain some idea of the extent to which they were writing as representatives of the dominant classes in society and also to determine their attitudes to their own and other social classes.

Over 150 volumes were examined. They were all on the subject of English History and there was at least one which was printed in each decade of the period 1800–1914. Inevitably, however, a majority of books dated from the later years of the period since more were published then in response to the stimulus of the growth of popular education after the Forster Act of 1870. Moreover, a proportion of history textbooks were not available even at the Bodleian Library or the British Museum. Although the law compelled the publishers of textbooks to offer copies to these institutions, lack of space apparently prevented their acceptance at certain periods during the last century. The fact that only three of the books date from the period 1810–20, while eighteen date from the period 1870–80 shows the difficulties in obtaining representative samples of textbooks throughout the period and the inadvisability of analysing such samples statistically. Furthermore, the fact that a book was published at a certain

---

[1] Knight (1865), preface p. iv.
[2] Hearnshaw (1914), preface p. v.

[14]

date does not mean that it was in use only for a brief period after that date. Mrs Markham's history which first appeared in 1819 was still being reprinted in 1874, and similar success was enjoyed by Lady Callcott and Miss Magnall among others. For this reason books which had a particularly wide sale or influence are marked with an asterisk in the Bibliography.

The methods by which the selected attitudes were examined was largely determined by the nature of the textbooks themselves. Since they have claims to being, in however minor a way, literature, and since the opinions which they express can usually be detected by examining choice of words and subject matter, the methods of literary criticism appeared more suitable on the whole than those of statistical analysis. Certainly an attempt to compare attitudes to a selected range of topics in three groups of ten books each drawn from the periods 1800–33, 1833–70 and 1870–1914 had to be abandoned when it became obvious that the attitudes to be found in them could only be fitted neatly into categories at the cost of absolute accuracy. However, the results of this attempt, such as they were, were used to ensure that impressions gained by literary study were not misleading. Every book was accordingly examined on its own merits and also as one of a group dating from a particular period. Each of the general attitudes under investigation was associated with a group of events or personages of English history, the treatment of which might be expected to furnish some clue as to the writer's point of view. Once note had been taken of particular opinions, each book was roughly classified as to the degree to which it adopted what is now known as the Whig interpretation of history or showed signs of Toryism, the degree of its Protestant or Catholic bias, and the extent to which it exhibited nationalistic attitudes. In some books the amount of space devoted to social and economic history was noted and compared to the total number of pages in the book. In other books this procedure proved unsuitable since they were aiming to give only a mere skeleton of facts. Since bias can be exhibited by the facts which are left out as well as by those which are included, notable omissions were recorded, though the significance of these is doubtful. Lack of space undoubtedly accounts for some omissions. Also the books which were published in the first two decades of the nineteenth century cannot be expected to include reference to Peterloo, e.g. and it is a moot point as to the date in the century when this event, which was undoubtedly a painful one to relate for many of the authors, can reasonably be expected to be included.

Next the views collected were grouped together and examined in chronological order to discover first whether there was any uniformity in the attitudes expressed, and secondly whether they do appear to change during the period 1800–1914. An effort was made to discover whether there was any significant difference between the opinions expressed in history textbooks which were to be used in popular education—that is, the history readers adapted to the codes of the Education Department or published for voluntary bodies, such as the National Society—and those in use in public and independent schools and colleges. This investigation proved to be difficult, however, because it seems likely that teacher-training colleges or normal schools used the same history textbooks as the latter. For instance, the popular *A School and College History of England* (1860) was written by J. C. Curtis who was vice-principal and lecturer in history at the Training College, Borough Road. It is extremely likely, therefore, that this book would be used as the basis of history lessons given by his students when they went out to teach in the schools of the British and Foreign Schools Society. Moreover, even where textbooks had been provided, the good teacher was urged to use them for reference only: 'Let the book, however, be treated as supplementary and wholly subordinate to the oral lessons, and be used for reference and home study mainly, and then it falls into its proper place.'[1] This would suggest that it would be unwise to draw too great a distinction between attitudes in textbooks intended for use in the various types of schools and colleges because in practice the books were interchangeable. However, books have been classified as suitable for senior pupils over thirteen years of age (S) or as suitable for junior pupils (J) to give some idea of the standard of maturity and judgment for which the book was written.

The opinions which emerged from a study of the history books had, of course, to be related to those current in society at the time. This was no easy task since Victorian England was essentially a free society and proud of the intellectual freedom which made it a refuge to the persecuted from the rest of Europe. In such a milieu a wide variety of opinions flourished and it would be unrealistic to expect all of them to be reflected in history textbooks. It is, therefore, a matter of judgment as to how far any of these might reasonably be expected to appear in any particular book, and a matter of conjecture as to the reasons for omission or inclusion. Indeed, we encounter here an intensification of the difficulty experienced already in

---

[1] *Lectures on Teaching*, by J. G. Fitch (1885), p. 372.

the detection and classification of opinions in the history textbooks. The recognition and selection of this material is admittedly the product of bias resulting from personal prejudices or from the preconceptions of the modern world. Those engaged in historical research must be open to the accusation that they judge past ages by the standards of their own, and where they seek to point the bias of others, the accusation must carry greater weight. However, since the study of how ideas are passed on to the rising generation is of continuing importance, the effort to pursue it must be made. The following work is intended to be a small step to that end.

CHAPTER I

Opinions about Social Class

'But it is a great comfort to think we need not be
afraid of being transported, for you know gentlemen
never steal sheep.'[1]

W HAT sort of children were expected to read the books and why ? It
is essential to consider these questions in relation to history textbooks in order to illuminate the opinions which they contain.
Certainly differing answers to them predominated at various times in the
nineteenth century. In the early years there were many who shared the view
of Lord Chesterfield that history was particularly a subject for the upper
classes to study: 'An intimate knowledge of history, my dear boy, is
absolutely necessary for the legislator, the orator and the statesman, who
thence deduce their morals and examples, speaking and judging of the
present, and by it the past, prognosticating the future.'[2] By the time of the
First World War few considered the subject to be suited mainly to the
highest ranks of society. As perceptive contemporaries noted, the movement towards manhood suffrage, finally attained in 1918, meant that every
man must be trained to take his part in the government. In a letter printed
in *History*, J. W. Headlam expressed his view that the war was making it
plain that education in general and the study of history in particular must
be extended to all classes of society: 'The child must be brought up not
only as a gentleman or as a scholar, or an athlete, but as the responsible
member of a free, self-governing community'.[3] This shift in readership
from the gentry and middle-class to the working-class child in the elementary school inevitably had its impact not only on the type of book
which was produced, but on the type of author which produced it. This, in
turn, resulted in a revolution in opinions about the various classes of society
which were expressed in history textbooks.

---

[1] Markham (1874), p. 23.
[2] *Letters from a Nobleman to his Son*, by Lord Chesterfield (1810 ed.), p. 174.
[3] 'The Effect of the War on the Teaching of History', *History*, New Series 3
(1918), p. 14.

At the beginning of the nineteenth century, and for many years afterwards, political power in England was still largely in the hands of an elite of aristocratic landowners, whose families dominated the government, the armed services and the Church. Promotion in these spheres accordingly tended to depend less on aptitude and education than on family influences and connection. As Dr Hans has shown in an analysis of the differing educational backgrounds of a group of leading men of the eighteenth century, the traditional education for the aristocratic elite was a private tutor followed by further studies, often of a rudimentary nature, at one of the great public schools, perhaps Eton, and a year or two at Oxford or Cambridge.[1] The academies which flourished in the later part of the century certainly offered a more complete education, but they were patronised less by the aristocracy and gentry than by those who wished their children to join the upper ranks of society by developing their talents to the full. In these circumstances it is not surprising that education in general and the study of history in particular came to be valued partly as a training for statesmen and partly as a means of producing the cultivated gentlemen for whom learning was also a pleasure. We have already noted Lord Chesterfield's comment on the value of an understanding of history.[2] This view is commonly expressed elsewhere, notably by Hannah More, who in her advice to the only daughter of the future George IV, declared: 'History, which is the amusement of other men, is the school of princes'.[3] The idea that history was 'an innocent and elegant amusement'[4] and a means of acquiring a high level of mental cultivation persisted late into the nineteenth century. Lord Derby, in a speech at the opening of Liverpool College in 1871, lamented that education had become too often a narrow training to fit the pupil for his work and duties in later life: 'In the present day we are a little too apt in all classes to look upon ourselves for mere machines for what is called "getting on" and to forget that there are in every human being faculties which cannot be employed, and many wants which cannot be satisfied by that education.'[5]

Some time before this a new attitude to the study of history and other subjects had emerged, however. A writer in the *Educational Guardian*

---

[1] *New Trends in Education in the Eighteenth Century*, by N. Hans (1951), pp. 26–7.
[2] See p. 18.
[3] More's *Hints* (1805), p. 71.
[4] *Systematic Education*, by Shepherd, Joyce and Carpenter (1815), p. 241.
[5] *National Schoolmaster* (1872), p. 15.

remarked that history was no longer 'a mere amusement' as it had been 'in the days of our fathers'.[1] During the course of the nineteenth century representatives of the middle and upper classes were able to reform public schools and some of the grammar schools so that they provided a suitably useful and socially acceptable education for their children. This movement received added impetus after the Reform Act of 1832 which confirmed and enforced the rise to political power of the professional and commercial middle classes. A series of reforms opened up new avenues for advancement in spheres of employment, some of which had hitherto been reserved for those with aristocratic connection. The Queen's scholarships, founded in 1846, gave grants to those who wished to train as teachers; in 1871 the Civil Service was opened to competitive examination, and even the sale of commissions in the army was stopped by Cardwell's reforms so that promotion depended more on training and ability. At the same time the beginning of the College of Preceptors (1853) and the Oxford and Cambridge local examinations (1859) encouraged those who saw educational qualification as a means of getting on in the world. Indeed so extensive was the triumph of *laissez-faire* competitive doctrines that there were feelings that the process was going too far. Thomas Huxley was reported in the *National Schoolmaster* as attacking those who said that people were managing to get an education above their station: 'They heard that argument more frequently from the representatives of the well-to-do middle classes, and coming from them it struck him as peculiarly inconsistent—as the one thing they admire, strive after, and advise their own children to do, was to get on in the world and, if possible, to rise out of the class in which they were born into that above them.'[2] To those who took the utilitarian view of education the study of history appeared necessary to fit the pupil for some particular career, or, as Herbert Spencer believed, to elucidate for him the 'causes of social progress'.[3]

However, some writers used utilitarian arguments to justify the denial of any education whatsoever to the poor. As late as 1854 a writer in the *Educational Times* declared that: 'Whether it be a peasant or a prince, the great principle of utility must be the best; and therefore that education which is manifestly unsuited to the wants and requirements of the working class must unfit them for duties to which, as members of society they are

---

[1] *Educational Guardian*, vol. IV (1861), p. 65.
[2] *National Schoolmaster* (1871), pp. 314–15.
[3] *Essays on Education*, by H. Spencer (1911 ed.), p. 26.

all more or less liable'.[1] The writer went on to criticise those who were not only teaching the poor to read and write, but to appreciate other subjects (presumably including history). 'Little do the advocates of this system think that they are doing as much to overturn the existing state of this country as the most levelling doctrines ever introduced, as by the forming of false tastes and feelings incompatible with the position of the holder.' However, the prevailing view in the later nineteenth century was that since 'their haste, their irresponsibility, their openness to deception and their inevitable ignorance' made the lower classes dangerous to the order and prosperity of society, they must be educated to different ways.[2] The Education Act of 1870 was partly the result of the realisation that the Reform Bills of 1832 and 1867 had made the prospect of manhood suffrage more imminent. The expansion of popular education which followed the Education Act of 1870 was in part designed to educate a future electorate to use its political power more wisely.

Another factor in the growth of education for the working classes during the nineteenth century was the belief, supported by the arguments of Malthus and other political economists, that they were not only dangerous to public order but feckless and immoral also. Since all citizens were adjudged to have an equal chance in the competition of a *laissez-faire* society, those who failed were often considered careless, lazy and improvident. Moreover, they were thought to be too eager to take the charity of others. In the earlier years of the nineteenth century the Speenhamland system, by which outdoor relief was granted to the recipient according to the price of bread and the number of children in the family, was held to encourage the dependence of the poor as well as their feckless tendency to breed.[3] In 1834 it was accordingly abolished by the Poor Law Amendment Act which restricted poor relief to those who entered the workhouse where conditions were supposed to be worse than those outside. Even this was considered too lenient to the poor by some contemporaries. In the Britain of 1894 the result of the poor-rate and other charity was declared to be 'demoralising'. It meant that 'people leave their work, they cringe, they lie and degrade themselves' in order to obtain relief.[4] The leading voluntary societies who began popular education in England, of which the British

---

[1] *Educational Times* (1854), p. 302.
[2] *The Economist* (1848), quoted in *Ideas and Beliefs of the Victorians* (1947), p. 293
[3] See also p. 33-4.
[4] Quoted in *The Victorians*, edited by J. Evans, p. 45.

and Foreign Schools Society and the National Society are the most notable, had as part of their aim to reclaim the poor from the dangers of immorality as well as impiety. This tradition was carried on throughout the century by denominational and later by Board Schools. It is expressed at its noblest by the Earl of Shaftesbury: 'We owe to the poor of our land a mighty debt. We call them improvident and immoral and many of them are so: but that improvidence and that immorality are the results in great measure of our neglect and not a little of our example.'[1]

A significant adjunct to the spread of education to all classes of society in the nineteenth century is the changing social and professional status of the writers of textbooks themselves. Very few of them were drawn from the upper classes. Only one, Philip, the fifth Earl of Chesterfield (Lord Mahon), was a peer. He was a scholar of some note and his work was really intended for the adult reader though it was recommended for use in schools. Bishop Davys held the see of Peterborough, but he had little significance in national as opposed to ecclesiastical affairs. His book began as a piece of journalism, being published as a series of letters in *The Cottagers Monthly Visitor*. Lady Maria Callcott was the daughter of a rear-admiral and married as her second husband Augustus Callcott, R.A., who was subsequently knighted. She began writing at a time when she and her first husband, a captain in the navy, were undergoing a period of financial stringency. Although well connected, she did not belong to the highest ranks of society. Nor, we may conjecture, did the 'Lady' whose *Notes on English History* was published for 2d. in the middle of the nineteenth century by John Heywood. Even Mrs Markham (Mrs Elizabeth Penrose) who wrote as if she and her children were members of the landed gentry was in fact the wife of a clergyman. Although her family was well-to-do, she belongs firmly to the middle class. In reality she was a professional writer rather than a gifted amateur exercising her talents 'for art's sake'.

By far the largest group of authors whose textbooks are included in this study were professional writers to a greater or lesser degree. A few of them were literary figures of some importance in their own day. At the end of the eighteenth century a new edition of Dodsley's history, which so enraged Mrs Trimmer, made its appearance. Robert Dodsley had, in fact, been dead since the middle of the century so that the part of his work which deals with the later years of George III must be by a later and more radical hand. We know that Dodsley was a publisher and author, the

---

[1] Quoted in *Ideas and Beliefs of the Victorians* (1949), p. 100.

patron and friend of Johnson, and, according to his brother James, the person who suggested the compilation of a dictionary to the great doctor.[1] Dodsley's history was a satirical work which was intended for the adult reader and it is only included as a textbook because it provides an interesting example of the sort of attitudes which were generally disapproved of in history textbooks and because Mrs Trimmer thought that some parents might allow their children to study it. It is perhaps significant that the 1826 edition of Dodsley's history is a partially bowdlerised version which imparts a certain amount of serious information in the footnotes.

William Cobbett, the author of the *History of the Protestant Reformation* wrote, like Dodsley, primarily for an adult readership. However, his work was occasionally recommended for study in school and since it is one of the few histories written by an author of radical views in the early nineteenth century, it has been included as a contrast to more orthodox and conservative works. Cobbett was the self-educated son of a labourer. He engaged in journalism and politics and it is for his work in these fields that he was chiefly remembered after his death in 1835.

Another of the well-known literary figures of the nineteenth century who wrote history textbooks was W. S. Ross. He was born in 1844 in Galloway, a tailor's son. Thanks to the sacrifices of his mother, he received a good education and became a schoolmaster. Soon, however, he decided to enter the ministry (1864). Even before this he had begun to write for newspapers and journals and when overwork brought on a breakdown and a revulsion from religious belief, he turned to writing as a career. His historical and romantic novels, such as *Mildred Merloch* and *Harp of the Valley* enjoyed some success and he was offered a job by the firm of Thomas Laurie for whom he produced textbooks on Latin, Maths and Grammar. In 1872 he took to publishing on his own account. Ross enjoyed many violent clashes with clerical enemies as well as many warm friendships with those who appreciated his atheist views. His friend and biographer, G. G. Flaws, claimed that in these encounters 'his pen became a barbed weapon and his ink as though a foeman's blood'.[2] Moreover he joined battle with another writer of textbooks—Farr—who in *Pilgrim Battles, Cross and Crescent* defended the crusaders and Christianity in general from the attacks of 'Saladin', Ross's *nom de guerre*. Ross was for a time secretary of the Lambeth Radical Association, but eventually eschewed all party allegiance,

---

[1] Boswell's *Life of Johnson* (1925 ed.), p. 59.
[2] *Sketch of the Life of Saladin* (1885), p. 8.

and contented himself with being the editor of *The Secular Review* which he began in 1884. Later he engaged in a furious controversy against a fellow atheist, Bradlaugh, whom he bitterly opposed on the subject of birth control, arguing that it might deprive the world of many an unborn genius.[1] Although Ross began life in humble circumstances, he rose to be a respected member of the middle class, and it is interesting to see how far his very decided views did or did not appear in his textbooks.

A writer of quite a different kind was Charlotte M. Yonge. She came of a military family—her father served at Waterloo—though her grandfather was a vicar and Charlotte inherited a strongly religious strain. She was a prominent follower of the Oxford movement; one of her books was entitled *Gleanings from Thirty Years Intercourse with the Rev. John Keble*. Her life was spent in quiet domesticity during which she wrote numerous novels and books on religious and historical subjects. She had some experience of teaching in the local parish school, but she remained primarily a writer. The same is true of her contemporary and friend, Elizabeth Missing Sewell. According to her autobiography,[2] she was born in 1815 into a middle-class family—her father was a clergyman—and like Miss Yonge became an acquaintance of Keble and Newman at Oxford. Like Miss Yonge also she began to write works of fiction, such as *Amy Herbert* (1844), and books on general religious topics such as *What can be done with our Young Servants?* (1873) and *Passing Thoughts on Religion* (1860). However, Miss Sewell's practical efforts as an educationalist were much more daring than those of her friend, and in 1852 she opened a school for girls on the Isle of Wight where she passed the latter part of her very long life. It is perhaps worthy of note that her brother founded Radley College.

A final example of a well-known literary figure who was connected with a history textbook is Rudyard Kipling. However, although his is credited with being the co-author of the *School and College History of England* by the publisher, it seems that he merely contributed the poems on English history which enliven it. The text is by C. R. L. Fletcher, though no doubt Kipling sympathised with the opinions which it contains.

It is impossible to trace the real professions of many of the other writers. Justin McCarthy is well known as Parnell's successor as leader of the Irish Nationalist Party. He was also the friend of W. S. Ross. Other writers were, from their titles, clergymen, though whether they practised

---

[1] Hithersay and Ernest (1887), p. 28.
[2] Edited by Eleanor M. Sewell (1907).

their vocation through work in the parish or the school is not always clear. The Rev. Mr Cooper, the Rev. Dr Brewer, the Rev. James White, the Rev. George Bartle, the Rev. Thomas Milner, all come into this category. Several of these part-time professionals produced books on a wide variety of subjects. For instance, Leonard Schmitz, who was a schoolmaster, produced works on Greek, Latin, Geography and German as well as history.

In fact one of the more interesting features of the social background of textbook authors is that by mid-century teachers of all kinds were predominating. To name but a few, Airy was a member of H.M. Inspectorate, Adams was headmaster of Riding Hons Street School, Carter was a headmaster of New College School, Curtis was a lecturer at Borough Road Training College, Livesey was a lecturer at Hammersmith Training College, Tait was a master at Clifton College, and Morris at Liverpool College where he taught classics. The *Jack Readers* were edited by Hayward, a headmaster at a Birmingham Council school. A feature of publishers' blurbs, in the latter part of the century especially, is the care they devote to informing the reader of the professional qualifications, in the way of degrees and teaching experience, which the writer enjoys. The positions held by Hearnshaw, Professor of History at King's College, London, Conan and Kendall, Professors of History at Wellesley College, and S. R. Gardiner, Fellow of Merton College, Oxford, are indications that there was a distinct move towards a more academic and less literary approach by 1914. Many of the books in use by that date were, therefore, written by people who had not only a good professional training in the study of history, but also experience of teaching in the public and independent schools for middle-class children as well as in the council and voluntary schools where working-class children were educated.

At the beginning of the nineteenth century, in contrast, it appears that authors were writing with the children of the gentry much in mind. Baldwin, writing in the preface[1] of his *History of England for the use of Schools and Young Persons*, asserted: 'I hold that particulars of which an accomplished gentleman and scholar may without dishonour confess that he has no recollection, are a superfluity with which it is quite unnecessary to overload the memory of a child.' Pinnock, whose work was published in 1822, also suggested that the study of history had certain enjoyable and improving qualities quite apart from any practical use, for it served to

---

[1] Baldwin (1812), p. v.

amuse the imagination and interest the passions.[1] To some of the writers of the early nineteenth century it seemed that one of their chief tasks was to prepare the children of the leisured classes so that in later years history could be a pleasant hobby—'to store the young mind with facts from history: and in so pleasing a form as to increase thirst for deeper knowledge as years ripen their understanding'.[2] Moreover, it is a characteristic of this group of 'genteel' authors that they frame their work as a series of stories for or conversations with their own children. Lady Callcott, for instance, claimed that she had written her history 'nearly as I would tell it to an intelligent child' because 'I want my dear Arthur to learn well the great lesson of loyalty as well as liberty'.[3] Among the histories which are written in the form of dialogue between children and author are those of Mrs Markham and of Anne Rodwell.

Mrs Markham's history in particular is an interesting example of the way in which authors of the early part of the nineteenth century were sure of the social standing of their readers and took for granted that it was usual to stay within one's own social group. At one point when Mrs Markham is explaining something of the legal system to her children, George remarks: 'But it is a great comfort to think we need not be afraid of being transported, for you know gentlemen never steal sheep.'[4] The truth of this assertion is not questioned, though it is explained in such a way as to leave no doubt that the upper classes are not only fortunate in their material circumstances but also morally superior to the poor: 'Because their temptations to it are not so great: besides it is to be hoped that we have a better knowledge of what is right and wrong than these poor creatures.' Later it comes as a shock to Richard to learn that anyone has ever dared to marry out of his social station. He asks: 'How could Queen Catherine marry a Welsh gentleman? I though queens and princesses only married kings and princes.' However, his mother is able to reassure him: 'It is best for all persons to marry in their own rank in life. Catherine's ill-assorted match brought her into general contempt.'[5]

Although as the century progressed, authors could no longer assume that they were writing for the members of one social class and that the highest, the ideal of history as a subject which should be studied for its

---

[1] Pinnock (1822), p. 2.
[2] Rodwell and Corner (1844), p. vi.
[3] Callcott (1872), p. 272.
[4] Markham (1874), p. 23.
[5] Markham (1874), p. 185.

own sake as a means of pleasure survived. Miss E. M. Sewell, in her *Catechism of English History*, stressed the need for facts to be learnt 'which must be fixed in the memory if a taste for history is to be cultivated'.[1] Later Miss Rolleston claimed that her aim in writing was to encourage 'the pursuit of historical science'.[2] However, the insistence on high academic standards and the study of history for its own sake in the later nineteenth century may be connected more with the growth of a 'scientific' school of historians, who, influenced by German examples, demanded high standards of accuracy in the writing of history, than with the 'aristocratic' view of history which had prevailed in the past.

Even where history was referred to as a useful rather than merely a pleasurable study in the early nineteenth century, it was thought by some authors of textbooks to be of use mainly to the upper classes of society. The Rev. Mr Cooper, writing about 1830, declared that: 'History, of all other studies, is the most necessary for the man who is to live in the world.'[3] He goes on to imply that the statesman may gain vicarious experience from the examples of history. Later in the nineteenth century Farr also saw history as a way in which those who were to undertake the 'duties of active life' were enabled to learn from the mistakes and triumphs of the past.[4] These views presuppose that the writer is addressing pupils who will form members of the ruling class and are, not surprisingly, found only in textbooks which could be used in public or grammar schools. However, in the second half of the nineteenth century authors apparently began to appreciate that the study of history could be of utilitarian value not only to the upper ruling classes but also to the aspiring middle classes who hoped to improve their position by ability and industry. A whole series of histories appeared which were obviously and openly designed to enable the student to pass examinations. Ince and Gilbert's *Outlines of English History* appeared in 1859 and was produced with an eye to the examination of the Royal Society of Arts. Collier's *History of the British Empire* was directed towards the Civil Service examinations, and books by Bartle (1865), Pringle (1870), Rose (1873), Murby (*c.* 1871) and Morison (1901) were concerned, as their titles and publishers' blurbs denote, with the examinations necessary to pass the Oxford and Cambridge local examinations in history. Many textbooks of the period are in reality mere

---

[1] Sewell (1872), preface.
[2] Rolleston (1911), p. vi.
[3] Cooper (1830), p. 30.
[4] Farr (1856), p. 4.

lists or summaries of facts collected for the same purpose. Indeed, reviewers of these books in educational journals sometimes remarked on this and lamented the dismal nature of their task. The *Educational Review* for 1900, while offering a prize of five guineas to the best list of books for use in the Junior Local Examinations, declared that: 'A History of England for High schools and Academies' was particularly welcome. One feature in particular destroys almost its examinational but enormously increases its educational value: it wholly ignores many minor names and details.[1] Even Fearenside's *Matriculation History*, a work which appears tedious by modern standards, was hailed as picturesque and vivid in comparison to the rest.[2] Earlier a reviewer in the School Board Chronicle had criticised Murby's history for presenting the facts in a 'heavy and dry manner',[3] while Morris's work was also damned as a 'cram history' in the *Saturday Review*.[4]

Towards the end of the nineteenth century while some writers were continuing to concentrate on helping the ambitious middle-class pupil on his upward path, others found an outlet for their talents in works designed for use in popular education. In the early nineteenth century only the occasional daring radical historian had claimed to be addressing the working class or speaking on its behalf. Cobbett, for instance, in his *History of the Protestant Reformation* stated bluntly that: 'It is not for the rich and powerful of my countrymen that I have spoken, but for the poor, the persecuted, the proscribed.'[5] Such works were rarely used in schools, however. History was often taught in voluntary schools for the poor towards the middle of the nineteenth century until the Revised Code of 1861 led to it being regarded as superfluous in comparison to the three Rs for which a government grant was received. In the 1870s history was once again reinstated in favour as a subject for the upper standards and since the teaching of it was found to be unsatisfactory, the aid of history reading books was usually made compulsory in Board Schools.[6] In the Code of 1900 the subject itself was made compulsory for the first time. These changes led to the publication of a spate of textbooks designed expressly for use in elementary schools. Usually authors wrote historical readers and

---

[1] *Educational Review* (1900), p. 305.
[2] Ibid., p. 162.
[4] *School Board Chronicle* (1 April 1871), p. 226.
[4] Ibid. (9 March, 1872), p. 119.
[5] Cobbett (1824), p. 478.
[6] *L.C.C. Report on the Teaching of History* (1911), p. 11.

announced on the frontispiece that their work was prepared in conformity with the latest Code issued from the Department of Education. One of the earliest of these is Legge's *A Reading book of English history for the use of pupil teachers and the upper classes of Elementary and other schools.* Other books in this category included *Leading events in English History adapted to the Code of 1871* by W. B. Adams, Livesey's *Primer of English History* (1871), and the Royal School Series (published by the National Society, 1874–5). The revised codes of the next decade resulted in another spate of activity to meet the demands of a changing syllabus. Blackwoods, Cassells, Nelson's, Chambers and Seymours were among publishing houses that produced historical readers in the 1880s. The Royal School Series went on being produced and the talented Miss Charlotte M. Yonge produced her *English History Reading Books* in 1880. During the last decade of the nineteenth century the flow of readers continued. The *Avon Readers,* the *Raleigh History Handbooks,* the *Warwick Readers* and Miss Yonge's response to the Code of 1890, the *Westminster Reading Books,* all date from this time. By the early years of this century, there were reissues of older readers rather than new ones, since the ending of the system of payment by results had meant that no new codes were issued and schools were accordingly at liberty to keep the same history syllabus as long as they wished. Nevertheless, the firm of Pitman issued the *King Edward Readers* in 1901 and the *Tower Readers* in 1911. Other sets of readers which seem to date from this time are the *Jack Readers* (1905), and the *Cambridge Readers* (1911).

However, even if books came to be written for the working-class child they were rarely written by an author of the working class, as we have seen. The almost completely middle-class origins of the authors of textbooks considered in this study is perhaps reflected in their attitudes to the gentry and aristocracy. They are not often mentioned and when they are, the reference is not always complimentary. Certainly no tinge of Disraelian reverence for the aristocracy was allowed to creep in. As we have seen, Mrs Markham made a spirited defence of the gentry's moral superiority,[1] but this was under attack elsewhere right through the nineteenth century. For most writers their objectionable feature was frivolous extravagance. For instance, the author of *Allison's Guide* drew attention to the extravagance of Richard II's court as a cause of the peasants' revolt,[2] and to the

---

[1] See earlier, p. 26.
[2] Allison (*c.* 1880), p. 188.

extravagance of Elizabeth and the nobility who surrounded here.[1] A few writers commented on the avarice of the aristocracy at the time of the Reformation: 'Many profligate and unworthy nobles were enriched with the spoils of the church.'[2] Moreover, Baldwin, who has some claim to belong to the 'genteel' school of writers, implied that the commercial classes were rather more trustworthy than the aristocracy. He wrote of Edward III at Calais, when the King is threatening to hang the burgers: 'How strange that a prince that behaved so humanely to people of rank, should have been so harsh and unrelenting to honest citizens.'[3] Some writers also noted the insensitivity of the upper classes to the sufferings of others. In one account of Peterloo it was remarked that the use of the military 'excited the anger of very many *even* of the wealthier classes'[4] and Miss Corner, in describing the fight against the Repeal of the Corn Laws, declared: 'The system is defended by those who possess land, for which they endeavour to obtain as much rent as they can . . . producing such a frightful extent of misery to the manufacturing population that nothing but the poor rates could enable them to exist.'[5]

Finally, the landed gentry were depicted as a class in decline, out of touch with the demands of the modern world, and challenged by the shift in political power which came with the 1832 Reform Act. One author even saw William Pitt the Younger, who meets with almost uniform approval elsewhere, as a representative of this class. 'Pitt, although the greatest war minister we have ever possessed, looked upon money with a certain amount of scorn. The result was that while under his ministry we gained a large amount of glory, the National Debt grew to one-hundred-and-twenty-eight million pounds.'[6] However, commerce could not be long neglected: 'The rapid increase of wealth among the lower classes, the inevitable result of a growing commerce, called into existence a rival power, of itself more than adequate to the overthrow of ancient prejudices.'[7] Some authors commented on the part played by the Reform Bill in sealing the decline of the aristocracy: 'It limited their influence by admitting more largely the middle class and upper ranks of the working men to share in the

---

[1] *Allison* p. 321.
[2] Legge (1869), p. 75.
[3] Baldwin (1854), p. 64.
[4] Bright (1875), p. 1363.
[5] Corner (1885), p. 288.
[6] Jack (1905), vol. 3, p. 52.
[7] Gleig (1853), p. 522.

government of the country.'¹ In fact the aristocracy showed remarkable resilience and powers of survival after 1832, but this is nowhere remarked upon.

In contrast to the nobility and landed gentry, the middle classes received almost uniformly favourable treatment throughout the century in all types of books. It is true that Baldwin shows traces of an aristocratic outlook in his suggestion in connection with Walpole that those interested in commerce are likely to be uncultured and uninterested in politics: 'The object of his administration was to render the nation rich, commercial and pacific, a people of trade, uninfluenced by the love of literature or the love of liberty'.² Most writers in the later part of the nineteenth century, however, identified the commercial classes with the love of liberty from the time of Elizabeth I onwards. They also suggested that the Queen's reputation was linked with progress made by commerce in her reign: 'Queen Elizabeth was one of the greatest and ablest rulers that England ever had. During her reign of forty-five years the country made much progress in manufactures, and peace was, for the most part, maintained at home and abroad.'³ When describing the battle between King and Parliament, some writers pointed out that the merchant class was on the side of the latter and largely responsible for its triumph. 'The Commons were supported by most of the merchants and traders, and by all the puritans and those who desired alteration in matters of religion.'⁴ There is even the suggestion that the triumph of liberty in England was inevitable, so firmly linked is it to the dominance of the middle classes. '. . . But now that commerce was introduced liberty soon followed; for there never was a nation that was perfectly commercial that submitted long to slavery.'⁵

In some textbooks there is open pride at the progress of the middle classes as a triumph of civilisation. 'Thus it came about that England, which was once a land of savages, is now, as it were, the great shop or market of the world.'⁶ Elsewhere they were praised as the most essential part of Victorian England. 'Henceforward the new trading (or middle) class grew in influence and wealth until it became what it now is, the heart and brain of the nation.'⁷ It was even suggested at times that God had

---

¹ Morris (1883), p. 216.
² Baldwin (1812), p. 134.
³ Warwick (1895–6), vol. 6, p. 158.
⁴ *Cassells Simple Outline* (1884), p. 130.
⁵ Scott and Farr (1861), p. 280.
⁶ *Cassells Simple Outline* (1884), p. 10.
⁷ King Edward (1901), p. 75.

a special interest in England's commercial progress. 'The persecution of foreign protestants, by the over-ruling hand of God, proved of service to England, as many skillful artisans came hither and thus improved our manufactures.'[1] Some writers also asserted that never have the enterprising members of society been so free to better themselves as in their own day. Gladstone was praised for his reforms 'to abolish the power of long-favoured minorities',[2] and Miss Yonge remarked: 'We have looked through English history and find that there never was a time when ability, backed by industry and uprightness, would not raise a man to full power, renown and influence. This is more than ever the case now, when the means of learning are within reach of all, for there are no obstructions in the way.'[3]

Just as the 1832 Reform Bill was seen as marking the end of aristocratic power, so it seemed to many writers to begin an era of political as well as economic opportunity for the middle class: 'The middle classes had helped the Whigs to carry the Reform Bill and the victory rested with them.'[4] Another of this group, Ransome, noted that 'this reform was the natural result of the Industrial Revolution which had caused wealth and enterprise to the North of England and was the beginning of a new period in the nation's constitutional history'.[5] As a teacher in a Yorkshire college, Ransome had a particular reason for stressing the North. The Reform Bill of 1867 also came in for some comment as a means whereby the more enterprising members of Victorian society could be enabled to attain political influence. The author of the *Blackwoods Educational Series* wrote: 'For many years it had been felt that the Reform Bill of 1832 had not gone far enough, and that a great many intelligent English were still without votes and without influence on the legislation of the country.'[6]

There is an obvious difference between the respect accorded to the rising middle classes and the opinions concerning the lower classes in society in most of the textbooks. The very terms used to describe those who failed to take advantage of the opportunities of a *laissez-faire* society give an indication of the authors' attitudes. They are the 'lower orders'[7] or 'the

---

1 Curtis (1860), p. 69.
2 Hearnshaw (1914), p. 158.
3 Yonge (1880), vol. 5, p. 254.
4 Hassall (1901), p. 521.
5 Ransome (1890), p. 225.
6 Blackwoods (1883), vol. 3, p. 224.
7 Adams (1872), p. 33.

inferior ranks of society'.[1] Moreover, they are easily led—'deluded populace'.[2] Some authors were sympathetic to them and, like the Rev. Milner, hoped for an improvement in the lot of the 'dependent classes'[3] or 'brothers of low degree'.[4] Certainly by the end of the century the terms applied were in some cases less scornful, especially in books written with a view of use in state schools or by people with experience in them. They were referred to as 'the poor',[5] merely as 'the people',[6] or 'the working class'.[7] To the Radical Irishman, McCarthy, they were 'other human creatures'.[8]

Time and time again the textbooks throughout the century stressed the belief that the poor were not only slothful, but promiscuous, wasteful and generally self-indulgent. Bishop Davys set the keynote for the century when he denied the idea of equality in society because some members of it would always waste their resources while others increased them. 'If we were all equal today, if all the property in the country were to be equally divided amongst us, we should not be equal tomorrow.'[9] He went on to stress that it was no one's fault but the poor man's if he were wretched. 'We know too that many people are living in great wretchedness, and we hear them complain against the government: but we can see plainly enough that the government has no share in causing their misfortunes, but that they are frequently brought on by themselves; we see that sober and prudent people are generally thriving and prosperous, and that drunken and careless people are generally in a state of poverty.'[10] It should perhaps be remarked that Bishop Davys was writing at about the time of Peterloo.

Nowhere is the attitude to the poor shown by the textbook writers more plain than in their comments about the system of poor relief and the Poor Law Amendment Act of 1834. In the earlier part of the century the radical, Cobbett, looked back to the Middle Ages as a time when the Church had taken care of the poor. In his view the Elizabethan Poor Law, leading to the Speenhamland system, which others considered too lax by far, was a measure of great brutality: 'The indigent the Catholic Church had so tenderly gathered under her wings were now merely for asking alms, *branded*

---

[1] Cooper (1843), p. 164.
[2] Ibid. (1830), p. 188.
[3] Milner (1854), p. 791.
[4] Ibid. p. 652.
[5] Airy (1898), p 191.
[6] Avon (1895), p. 106.
[7] Morris (1882), p. 254.
[8] McCarthy *Modern England before the Reform Bill*, (1899), p. 323.
[9] Davys (1822), p. 254.
[10] Ibid. pp. 128–9.

with red hot irons and made slaves.'¹ This view of the treatment of the poor in the Middle Ages continued throughout the century amongst Catholic writers and a few others: 'Still corrupt as it was, the Catholic religion during the dark ages and the time of the Plantaganets had done some service. It had never held that one class of people was better than any other, and had always opened the priesthood to every class.'²

The vast majority of writers throughout the century and in all types of book, however, took the view that the old Poor Law, based on the Speenhamland system, was not too harsh, but too lenient: 'A race of freemen rapidly became a race of paupers. Improvident marriages, large families and the profligacy which is still so bad a feature of rural life were legally encouraged by the dole of each child, whether legitimate or not.'³ The Rev. James White described an even more lurid scene, rejoicing that after the 1834 Act 'no lazy pauper could lounge up to the poor houses and demand his week's allowance and loaves of bread in proportion to the children he had left at home. No dissolute woman could flaunt in insolent finery on the money she received for the keep of her illegitimate children.'⁴ Nor were pupils in elementary schools spared the details, for we find the author of the *King Edward Reader* depicting a pauper who managed 'to live a fairly comfortable life without work',⁵ and other readers contain references to the way in which the poor rate was squandered on strong men and women who were too idle to work.

Nearly all writers regarded the Poor Law Amendment Act of 1834 not only as necessary but as beneficial in its results. Some do, it is true, report that it did cause suffering among the poor or that it was *thought* by contemporaries to have done so, yet they all stress not only the saving in the poor rates but the 'moral' improvement in the lower classes which accompanied it. The suggestion is that the poor were incapable of improvement by themselves and had to have improvement forcibly administered to them: 'This law was thought cruel at the time, but although it is an unchristian act to allow anyone to starve, yet it is equally cruel to encourage habits of sloth and improvidence.'⁶ The financial advantages were stressed by writers who noted the fall in rates with approval.⁷

---

1 Cobbett (1822), para. 222.
2 Bullock (1861), p. 99.
3 Airy (1898), p. 473.
4 White (1860), pp. 783–4.
5 King Edward (1874), p. 158.
6 Cassells (1883), p. 367.
7 Fearenside (1901), p. 196.

[34]

The poor appear in many textbooks not only as idle and improvident, but also somewhat dangerous and insolent. This accords with the view of contemporaries, mentioned above, that one of the purposes of education was to 'civilise' the lower classes so that they need no longer be a danger. One author remarked that Simon de Montfort was helped by Londoners, 'a class of persons remarkable, even in those days for their impatience under the control of authority'.[1] The characteristic most commonly attributed to the people in revolt was that of 'insolence' or of not knowing their place. On the whole many writers were, as we shall see, not unfavourably disposed to the Peasant's Revolt of 1381. Yet even here they stressed the dangers of inflaming the poor. 'When the common people have got arms in their hands, and feel themselves masters, they are apt to run into the most outrageous excesses.'[2] The death of Wat Tyler was persistently justified on the grounds that he acted rudely or insolently. Various writers referred to 'his impudence to the king',[3] to the fact that he 'behaved himself insolently'[4] or 'rudely'.[5] Perhaps the most extreme example of this tendency is Mrs Markham's. 'Walworth, unable to endure the sight of this clown's insolence to his sovereign, drew his sword and felled him to the ground with a blow.'[6]

At other points also opinions were expressed which imply that the lower classes are easily led into violent action and therefore unready for democracy. The continuator of Hume described how they erupted into 'outrageous violence' and then returned to their former 'slavish condition' after the passing of the 1832 Reform Bill.[7] Fletcher noted how at the same time 'The Whigs, being weak in Parliament, did not scruple to appeal to the passions of uneducated people',[8] and Miss Yonge described how 'one lady was actually frightened to death' by the mob.[9] The Chartists were also used as examples of the volatile nature of the working class. They were held to be 'chiefly mechanics, labourers and others of the lower classes who were led by demagogues to desire a "People's Charter" '.[10] It is true that the author of *A History Written on a Plan of Lord Chesterfield* praised

---

[1] Gleig (1860), p. 115.
[2] Baldwin (1812), p. 70.
[3] Gill (1870), p. 25.
[4] Morris (1883), p. 133.
[5] *Royal Purse Series* (1898), p. 130.
[6] Markham (1874), p. 158.
[7] Hume (1875), p. 715.
[8] Fletcher and Kipling (1911), p. 225.
[9] Yonge (1880), Book 5, p. 236.
[10] Corner (1885), p. 300.

'the temperance of the mobs' at the time of the Chartist agitation,[1] but the prevailing attitude even to the end of the century is that the working class was not to be trusted. As Hearnshaw remarked in a book which was published as late as 1914: 'It has yet to learn how to use its power; to educate itself in political problems, and to acquire discipline, restraint and large views.'[2]

It is this lack of confidence in the people at large that is perhaps reflected in the attitudes expressed by the writers towards the Education Act of 1870 (which did so much to encourage popular education). In every case where the Forster Act was mentioned, it was put forward as something to be welcomed. Attention was drawn to the sad plight of children in the past: 'But one hundred years ago very few children went to school at all. They were left to run wild and play about the streets until they began to work and often they went to work at a very early age.'[3] The *Jack Readers* (written by teachers in council schools) even went so far as to suggest that there were great shortcomings in voluntary schools before 1870: 'They had little money beyond that received from the government to spend on their schools, some of which were badly built, badly furnished and under-staffed.'[4] The effects of the Education Act upon the people was depicted in glowing colours. As Miss Yonge explained: 'A law has been made that all children must go to school and be well taught, so that we may all know what is wise and right and the best way of doing it.'[5] The suggestion was made that the children of the poor would receive moral as well as material improvement from education: 'The inmates of the poorest homes in Britain now lead a happier and better life; because they are more thoroughly educated.'[6] Few authors stressed the link between the Forster Act and the hope that the lower classes could be educated to enjoy their increasing political powers without breaking out into revolution, though there is the occasional hint at it: 'And as people cannot be good citizens without being well taught, Parliament has provided for the education of all children in the country.'[7] Even so there seems to have been a feeling among some writers that the children and their parents will carry the tradition of

---

[1] Cooper (1843), p. 239.
[2] Hearnshaw (1914), p. 173.
[3] *Chambers* (1901–4), vol. 2, p. 124.
[4] *Jack* (1905), p. 228.
[5] Yonge (1890), p. 114.
[6] *Chambers* (1901–4), p. 122 (vol. 6).
[7] Callcott (1872) p. 266.

working-class sloth and self-indulgence to the point of not appreciating or benefiting from the education offered. 'Thus learning was spread over all the land, and it is now the parents' own fault if their children are not able to read and write thoroughly at an age when they must begin to earn their daily bread.'[1]

Still it would appear that as the social status of readership and author changed, so did the references to the predominating class become more complimentary. Though they did in fact retain much of their power, the aristocracy and gentry were replaced by the commercial middle classes as objects of admiration and respect by the mid-nineteenth century. As the First World War approached, even the working class, once reviled as feckless and dangerous, were treated with more respect—not surprisingly since commercial convenience obviously dictates that no writer abuse his reader too openly. The authors of textbooks remained overwhelmingly middle class but they were often writing for the elementary school market where not only children, but teachers, too, came from the lower classes. Even allowing for this, however, there are a few indications that England was becoming less divided by nations of class stereotypes, such as 'the solid middle class' or 'the improvident poor'. How far such indications are based on little more than the desire of the propagandist not to alienate his audience may be decided by an examination of the political opinions also to be found in history textbooks of the period. These may give some clue as to the actual strength of any desire to mould the views of the 'future masters'.

---

[1] *Cassells* (1883) p. 383.

CHAPTER II

Political Opinions

'How thankful we ought to be . . . that we live under
a mild King and are governed by just laws.'[1]

TWO major objectives seem to be involved in the process of indoctrinating the rising generation with anti-revolutionary sentiments. To induce complacency at the present situation and disgust at those who would try to change it radically. Both these sentiments are discernible in the opinions on such topics as the monarchy and the progress of the nation and the constitution in history textbooks of the period 1800–1914. Moreover, it is not hard to select quotations from writers on the teaching of history who seem to advocate its use as propaganda against disruptive elements in society. For instance, London County Council Report of 1911, which is very moderate in tone, claimed that every child would have to fulfil two main functions of earning a livelihood and performing the duties of a citizen. For the latter, he should be taught of his heritage from the past and his responsibilities for the future. In particular he should be warned of the danger of abstract ideas and the 'party spirit of sensational journalism'.[2] Yet such evidence of the desire to indoctrinate should not be taken too seriously. Neither the L.C.C. nor the government was actually responsible for the selection of school textbooks.[3] This was in the hands of individual teachers, many of whom in voluntary or independent schools did not even owe their appointments to any local authority. Nor does the variety and complexity of political opinions in the textbooks themselves make it generally possible to assert that they follow any party line. Only where a topic aroused the strongest emotions does these seem to have been a form of voluntary censorship.

One of the most controversial of these topics was the monarchy. In the troubled period of the French revolutionary and Napoleonic wars and the years of economic and political instability which followed them in England,

---

[1] Davys (1822), pp. 53–4.
[2] *L.C.C. Report on the Teaching of History* (1921), pp. 8–9.
[3] See above, p. 10–11.

[38]

there were to be found writers such as Hannah More and Mrs Trimmer[1] who defended the institution and associated attacks on the characters of monarchs past and present with revolutionary feeling and intent. Nevertheless, there is abundant evidence that the behaviour of George IV in particular had brought the monarchy into such disrepute that its detractors were not only to be found in the radical party, but among many influential sections of opinion. Thus William Cobbett's condemnation of the Hanoverians—'not one of whom . . . has ever discovered symptoms of a mind much more sufficient to qualify the possessor for the post of exciseman'[2]— appears almost kindly in contrast to the abusive references to the late George IV and his successor which appeared in *The Times* on the occasion of the former's death in 1830.[3] Queen Victoria was certainly not immune from displays of anti-monarchical feeling. In the earlier part of the century Mill and Bentham wrote that monarchy was one of the worst forms of government. A popular outcry arose on the dismissal of Palmerston in 1851 for his refusal to consult or even inform the Queen of his policy as Foreign Secretary, and a new newspaper, the *English Republic*, was founded and flourished in the years 1851–5. Even the death of the Prince Consort in 1861 failed to draw any lasting sympathy to Victoria since she withdrew into seclusion away from the public engagements which might have restored her popularity. A pamphlet entitled 'What does she do with it?' drew attention to the view that her quiet existence hardly merited the large allowance which she received out of public funds. The setting up of a French Republic in 1870 was the signal for republican agitation in England which was backed by such notable figures as Sir Charles Dilke and Joseph Chamberlain.

However, Victoria's popularity made a swift revival. Coaxed back into the limelight by the Conservative Prime Minister, Disraeli, and signified by the Royal Titles Bill of 1876 which conferred upon her the title 'Empress of India', she allowed the Crown to be identified with the new imperialism. Although John Morley and others loudly protested against making loyalty to the Crown into a party political slogan and such left-wing figures as Keir Hardie continued their attack on the monarchy, Disraeli's manoeuvres proved of great advantage to the Crown's popularity as well as to the cause

---

[1] See p. 8–9.
[2] *The Opinions of William Cobbett* (1944 ed.), p. 91.
[3] Quoted in *The Crown and the Establishment*, by Kingsley Martin (1962), p. 27.

of imperialism. At Victoria's first jubilee of 1887 a wave of personal loyalty swept the country and this was repeated on the occasion of her diamond jubilee in 1897. The philosophical basis for renewed belief in the monarchical form of government was provided by Walter Bagehot in 1866. He argued that monarchy was necessary as an emotional binding force for all sections of society which must not be coldly analysed or criticised. 'As long as the human heart is strong and the human reason weak, royalty will be strong because it appeals to diffuse feeling, and Republic's weak because they appeal to the understanding. . . . Above all things our royalty is to be reverenced, and if you begin to poke about it you cannot reverence it.'[1]

For all the references to it in history textbooks, the republican attack on the monarch to which Bagehot was responding might never have existed. Only very rarely did there appear any criticism of the institution. Certainly Dodsley, whose work Mrs Trimmer dubbed 'altogether abominable', satirised it. He wrote in a pastiche of Biblical style of the errors of past rulers: 'And it shall come to pass when thou readest of the foolish kings that have ruled the land, then shall thy soul be troubled, and thou shalt say to thyself, how small a portion of sense sufficeth to govern a great kingdom.'[2] Then he apparently went on to hint that things were even worse now, in his own day, though the inference is open to various interpretations: 'But when thou readest of the Kings that were wise and great, then shall thy heart be glad, and thou shalt compare the times passed with the present and rejoice therein and laugh exceedingly.' Most shocking of all, Dodsley hinted that the pedigree of England's royal family was not above suspicion, for he concluded his genealogy of the Kings of England by pointing to "William Rufus, who was the son of William the Conqueror, who was the son of a whore'.[3] It is obvious, however, that Dodsley cannot have been widely used as a history book for children, except perhaps in a few radical homes. The interesting thing is that Mrs Trimmer was apparently afraid that it might be. Elsewhere one of the few dispassionate writers about the monarchy in general and the reigning sovereign in particular is W. S. Ross. His radical leanings are perhaps to be seen in the way in which he is forced to acknowledge his country's sterling qualities, but cannot bring himself to attribute them all to Victoria. 'For

---

[1] Quoted, Martin p. 167.
[2] Dodsley (1799), preface, p. ii.
[3] Ibid., p. 156.

we say it truthfully and with all simple sincerity that her reign is the most illustrious epoch in the annals of the world; and we are the most powerful, the wealthiest, the wisest, the most religious, the most moral and the happiest people that ever existed in this whirling ball, the earth. Of course, Victoria has little or nothing to do with all this. But we are a law-loving and loyal people: and, in the light of past experience, we are enthusiastically proud of any monarch who will condescend to behave herself or himself with the discretion and restraint of any ordinary mortal.'[1] The ironic tone of that extract is typical of much of Ross's work and perhaps illustrates the difficulty which a rebel or any man of unconventional views might find in expressing himself in a school textbook which has to sell on the open market.

For the most part, however, the pattern of attitudes to recent and contemporary royalty is constant throughout the period. Those monarchs who are near to the writer in time are singled out for special adulation, while those who are farther away in the past are treated more critically. In most cases it is the moral qualities of the sovereign which are singled out for praise, and where these are doubtful, as in the case of George IV, the authors falls back on praise of the achievements of the reign. There is, however, a general suggestion that approval of the monarch does depend on his morals or successful actions or, preferably, both. As Lady Callcott wrote of William III: 'King William knew that Kings are only to be better loved and obeyed than other men when they obey God themselves, and love mercy and do right and justice to their subjects, and that men and countries have a right to be free and to worship God as they please.'[2]

In some of the books published earlier in the century, George II received some praise, especially for his part at the Battle of Dettingen. One author wrote, that the troops were 'animated by the presence of their sovereign' on that occasion,[3] another inserted a long description of the battle, stressing the King's part in it.[4] Later writers virtually ignored this. There was praise for George III amongst the writers who had lived under his rule, such as Mrs Markham. She included a long account of his illness and the display of public rejoicing which accompanied a temporary recovery.[5] This praise continued intermittently throughout the century. Thus we find: 'A more virtuous, rational and pious king never sat upon

---

[1] Ross (1872), pp. 63–4.
[2] Callcott (1872), p. 229.
[3] Cooper (1830), p. 105.
[4] Hort (1822), p. 198.
[5] Markham (1874), p. 441.

the English throne; true to his God, his principle and his people.'[1]
However, by the end of the nineteenth century George III could be
depicted as 'A Tory King—the arch enemy to useful reforms, the stubborn
champion of popular prejudices'.[2] George IV fares even worse in the
history books, for few of them were written during his comparatively
brief reign and even those which date from that period, tactfully omit all
direct reference to his conduct. The best that can be said of him is that:
'As a man he had his faults; as a sovereign, few that ever sat upon the
throne of England deserve to be placed above him.'[3] Soon, however, he
was to be almost universally condemned. He was compared unfavourably
with his father: 'In morals he was as low as his father was high'.[4] and other
writers echoed the moral refrain: 'Like Henry VIII, happily without his
fondness for blood, or Charles II, unfortunately without his wit, he recalled
the two worst periods of our history by his disregard of the most sacred
ties and his addiction to sensual gratification.'[5] The elementary school
books also adopted this attitude to George IV. In one he was described as
'a king whom no one respected and whose death no one regretted',[6] and
in another 'a false bad man who lived in a loose life'.[7]

In contrast Queen Victoria was the subject of almost universal praise
during her reign. This appears to be partly due to the fact that, unlike
George IV, she was noted for her chastity and the happiness of her family
life. This is often stressed, and the loss of the Prince Consort is described
in fulsome terms, both immediately after his death and to the end of the
period: 'The universal grief at the loss of this great and good man, whose
admirable qualities were only beginning to be duly appreciated, almost
equalled the burst of sorrow experienced by the nation at the death of the
Princess Charlotte.'[8] Some tributes to Albert were expressed in verse:

> 'And with their Queen lamenting thousands weep
> As the sad dirge notes o'er the nations sweep,
> Telling, the tomb holds all of earth can Albert keep.'[9]

---

[1] Grimaldi (1871), p. 171.
[2] Edwards (1901), p. 68.
[3] Gleig (1856), p. 616.
[4] Morris (1883), p. 479.
[5] White (1860), p. 776.
[6] Warwick (1896), vol. 7, p. 192.
[7] *History of England Mostly in Words of One Syllable* (1907), p. 83.
[8] Bowes (1863), p. 24.
[9] Bourne (*c.* 1870), p. 31.

However, as one writer noted, the Queen's family life must continue: 'Four sons and five daughters, fair blossoms of happy married life, remain to console the royal lady, whose crown has now become a "lonely thralldom".'[1]

The Queen was also praised for her personal kindness and sometimes actual anecdotes of this were recounted. For instance, in a book published in the *Royal Purse Series* Queen Victoria was shown visiting a hospital and giving money to a poor child lying sick there. 'The poor mother did not like to spend it all on food. With part of it a Bible was bought, which the little boy still has.'[2] As her popularity recovered in her later years and immediately after her death, praise of the Queen seems to have intensified, especially in the elementary school readers, which are notably fulsome in their praise. The author of a Pitman reader remarked on her 'wonderful knowledge and grasp of political affairs' and then burst into verse:

> 'Her court was pure, her life serene,
> God gave her peace, her land reposed,
> A thousand claims to reverence closed,
> In her as Mother, wife and Queen.'[3]

In another reader there is a comparison between the problems faced at the beginning of the reign and Victoria's secure position at the end of it.[4] 'Her land was filled with distress and unrest, and tens of thousands were suffering from want. But the people loved her and trusted her, and their love and trust was amply repaid.' Perhaps the attitude of the readers generally to the Queen is summed up in the conclusion to a Cassells publication: 'So the English people love her now just as much as in the beginning and still go on singing God Save the Queen!'[5]

If the readers are perhaps the most obvious in their praise of the Queen, it is a common attitude in all books published near the turn of the century to approve Bagehot's view of the Crown as a unifying factor or as a representative of her people. Victoria was shown to be having a good effect on the nation as a whole: 'Her noble resolve to be good has helped to make her people good also.'[6] Another went so far as to assert that when

---

[1] Collier (1875), p. 330.
[2] (1891), p. 251.
[3] *Pitman* (1901), p. 212.
[4] *Tower* (1911), vol. 8, p. 136.
[5] *Cassells* (1884), *Stories from English History*, pp. 155-6.
[6] *Cambridge* (1911), vol. 1, p. 212.

the cry of 'Long live the King' was raised the people were praying for their own welfare as well as that of the sovereign.[1] Implicit in this view of the monarchy as a unifying and representative force is the realisation that the actual powers of the monarchy had declined during Victoria's reign, but this was obviously not considered suitable information for the child, though the author praised the Queen for her 'constitutional conduct'.[2] Indeed in one book, admittedly, one of the most conservative in tone, the powers left to the monarchy were stressed: 'Any very "revolutionary" proposal such as the abolition of either House of Parliament, the surrender of India and the colonies, the reduction of the Navy very far below the strength necessary to defend the Empire, might quite conceivably obtain for a moment a majority in the House of Commons, and though it is unlikely, it is just possible that the House of Lords might be tempted into accepting it. But *then* it would be the duty of the King to interfere, and to dismiss, at all costs, the Ministry which was rash enough to make such a proposal.'[3] Here the Crown is made to appear the last bastion against revolutionary changes for the future. Such an attitude to the monarchy is, however, almost unique. Most books concentrated, as we have seen, on the personal popularity of the sovereign as a binding and unifying force and suggest that it is well merited because of his or her moral worth. At the end of the period, hopes were being expressed that Edward VII would follow in the tradition established by his mother. 'Her son, Edward VII, bids fair to tread in her footsteps and has e'en now won a great praise as one who loves peace and will spare no pains to rid the world of the curse of war.'[4] Contemporaries seem to have found it hard to praise the moral virtues of one who had such tastes as Edward and accordingly fell back on his love of peace as a quality for which he could be commended.

Writers of textbooks were closely in accord with contemporary views when they showed the monarchy as able to adapt itself to suit the conditions of a new age, for the doctrine of progress, of change for the better, was an idea approved by men of all shades of opinion. As Basil Willey has suggested, by the end of the eighteenth century belief in a static, unchanging society had started to give way before a series of inventions and improvements which revolutionised the way of life in town and country.[5]

---

[1] *Jack* (1905), p. 242.
[2] Grimaldi (1871), p. 587.
[3] Fletcher and Kipling (1911), p. 228.
[4] *History of England Mostly in Words of One Syllable* (1907), p. 94.
[5] *Ideas and Beliefs of the Victorians* (1949), p. 40.

Even the essentially conservative Hannah More was speaking of that 'gracious progressiveness which is discernible in past events' by 1805.[1] The writings of Charles Darwin served to reinforce the impression that man had made progress in the past from animal barbarism to civilisation, and philosophers, notably Bentham, suggested that with proper care and organisation of society man could make further progress. The optimistic view of man's history can be traced in the writings of Macaulay, notably in the third chapter of his *History of England* when he compared the past with the present and drew the conclusion that the human species has advanced not only in a material sense but morally and intellectually as well. W. E. Forster also held that 'the law of humanity is progress'. He saw the teaching of history as a way of exhibiting the truth of this dictum and also of ensuring that material progress would lead to progress in virtue. This it need not necessarily do, as he was clear-sighted enough to realise.[2]

Certainly there was a strain of deep pessimism in nineteenth-century thought. Darwin's theories of evolution and the scientific study of the universe sometimes shattered the religious faith of the individual and induced a despair which sprang from a sense of the meaningless nature of existence. This is particularly clear in the poetry and novels of the period. Works such as Matthew Arnold's *Dover Beach* which pictured the world as 'a darkling plain swept with confused alarms of struggle and flight, where ignorant armies clash by night', and the novels of George Eliot and Thomas Hardy show traces of a fatalistic pessimism very different from the optimistic belief in progress exhibited elsewhere. In tone they lie closer to such eighteenth-century writers as Chapman who valued history because it gave man a sense of his own insignificance and the transience of worldly things. 'If we look back but a few years, they who acted on the theatre of human life are no more. What is become, it may be asked, of their deep-laid schemes, their ambitious projects, their anxious cares, their adored riches, their dazzling honours, their alluring pleasures. . . . If we look forward into futurity, where are we ourselves ? Gone, for ever gone, and the places of our abode know us again no more. . . .'[3] Chapman's austere view is in keeping with the tone of historical writing in the eighteenth century. Neither Gibbon, whose *Decline and Fall of the Roman Empire* dealt with a civilisation in decay, nor Hume assumed that the men

---

[1] More's *Hints* (1805), p. 200.
[2] 'The University a Trainer of Politicians', in *Aberdeen Rectorial Addresses* (1876), p. 219.
[3] *A Treatise on* Education (1790), p. 207.

of the past were in any way necessarily less happy or in other ways inferior to those of their own time.

The authors of history textbooks communicate very little of this pessimism. Perhaps this is attributable to the fact that they were writing for a rising and hopeful generation; perhaps to the desire to encourage a complacent attitude to the problems of the time. From the earliest years of the nineteenth century writers proclaimed that it was their happy task to trace the progress of mankind: 'Let us thankfully acknowledge the goodness of the supreme Moral Governor towards our forefathers and ourselves. Let us rejoice that the gloomy clouds of ignorance and superstition are rolled away; and that the storm of persecution and violence have passed by. That the sun of science, of freedom of religion, shines upon us in meridian glory.'[1] Thus Hort saw the progress of mankind as one towards religious peace and toleration and learning. Cooper, a near contemporary of his, also stressed the moral and intellectual advances of mankind. He wrote that history 'communicates to our enquiry the whole progress of improvement, the whole circle of knowledge and experience'.[2] Later in the century there was a tendency for the more material forms of progress, such as commercial success and national power in the world, to be singled out for mention. One who was a writer of markedly religious views claimed that his history would be of use as 'affording to youth the means of acquiring a sound knowledge of the chief events in the history of the country and an acquaintance with the rise and progress of those institutions to which, under Divine blessing, the country is indebted for its present exalted station'.[3] Other writers referred to the 'peace and prosperity' which England had come to enjoy,[4] 'advance in happiness and in self-respect' enjoyed by the British people,[5] and the fact that 'All departments of life have been characterised by progress and development'.[6]

Far from seeing the progress of the past as a foretaste of the change which might be expected in the future, however, the textbook writers in general exhibited a complacent opinion. Persistently throughout the century they drew the moral that the people should be grateful and co-operative for the benefits which they have received. The most outstanding example of this

---

[1] Hort (1822), p. 209.
[2] Cooper (1830), p. 3.
[3] Gleig (1853), p. v.
[4] Scott and Farr (1861), p. 768.
[5] Airy (1898), p. 319.
[6] Hassall (1901), p. 587.

occurs in Bishop Davys's history. Although the Six Acts which seriously hampered such 'traditional' rights as freedom of the Press and freedom to hold political or other meetings and present petitions, were still in force, he took a sanguine view of the progress of freedom: 'How thankful we ought to be that we live under a mild King and are governed by just and equal laws.'[1] Moreover, such benefits brought responsibilities for the people: 'It seems to me the duty of us all to be thankful for these blessings, and to consult the good of our country by loyal, peaceable and grateful obedience to those whom Providence has set over us.'[2] The bishop was at a loss to understand those who criticised the Tory government of his day when he looked to the dangers and cruelties of the past. 'How happy ought we to think ourselves that we are secure in these days from such cruelties and oppressions! There are many people now who complain of the want of liberty, and talk a great deal against rule and government, and seem full of anger and envy against everybody who is richer and greater than themselves. I cannot help seeing that the greater part of these complaints is made without reason at all. I am sure, if we would fairly consider these things, as we ought to do instead of murmuring and complaining, we should find a great deal indeed to be thankful for such cruelties as we read of in history could not be practised in our days.'[3] Few writers expressed such an extreme view as Bishop Davys, but they do manage to convey a general feeling that life is so pleasant now, compared with what it was like in the past that those who complain are ungrateful and deluded. Mrs Markham began her history by comparing the material and spiritual comforts of the British of her day with those of the past when there were no comfortable houses, convenient shops, roads, bridges or churches.[4] Likewise, the author of an elementary school reader, written later in the century, noted: 'We have seen England and Great Britain growing larger and larger, stronger and stronger, more and more free, more and more intelligent, until our Empire has risen to be the greatest, most powerful and most respected on the face of the globe . . .', and drew the moral: 'We must learn to love our country for what she has been in the past, and what she is now, and what she is destined to become in the future.'[5] The author of the *Chambers New Scheme Reader* also saw Britain as a country which is 'the

---

[1] Davys (1822), p. 10.
[2] Ibid. pp. 53–4.
[3] Ibid. pp. 113–14.
[4] *Markham* (1874), p. 11.
[5] *Blackwoods* (1883), vol 3, pp. 249–50.

happiest in the world'. He pointed out that the working-class home was now much more comfortable than ever in the past, and while admitting that misery still existed, concluded cheerfully: 'Even the adult artisan has now sufficient leisure to engage in outdoor amusements, to revel in the beauties of nature, to improve his mind by reading and study, if he be so disposed.'[1] The readers intended for use in elementary schools are in fact remarkable for the stress which they lay on progress and the need to be grateful for it, but they do not differ in attitude from the books which had long been used for the education of the upper classes. Miss Yonge, for instance, was brought up on Davys's history and always acknowledged her debt to it.[2]

However, there remained a small group of writers throughout the century who were not entirely convinced that the complacent tone of their contemporaries was justified, and expressed their fears of future developments. Sometimes this took the form of wondering whether the rising generation would be up to the standard of the old: 'It remains to be seen whether their descendants will prove worthy of the inheritance bequeathed to them and be able to hand on to their children as worthy a record of noble ideals and successful performance as their ancestors have left to them.'[3] Some conservatives had grave doubts about the wisdom of democracy and hinted at a bleak future for the country. One or two religious writers also felt disquiet about the state of the nation. Milner, whose book was published by the Religious Tract Society, admitted that society still exhibited 'many painful features' and that the bounds of error and vice as well as those of virtue and justice might be increasing, although he did end hopefully on the note that in England, thanks to the liberty of thought and action, there is usually a remedy for all grievances.[4] Charlotte Yonge also occasionally introduced a note of warning against too optimistic a view of the nation's political and material progress. For instance at one point she remarked: 'It is not by changes in the constitution of the country that times are made happy or prosperity achieved, but by living in the fear of God.'[5] One of the very few authors to make a sharp criticism of the idea of progress as such is T. F. Tout, who, while noting that the standard of living of the poor has gone up, added: 'But there is still too much dullness, monotony and lowness of aim among those comfortably off and too much

[1] *Chambers* (1901–5), vol 5, p. 206.
[2] *C. M. Yonge*, by E. Romanes (1908), p. 19.
[3] Ransome (1895), p. 1040.
[4] Milner (1852), p. 800.
[5] Yonge (1880), Book 5, p. 254.

[48]

abject misery and want among large sections of the community, to give us any room to look on nineteenth-century progress with undue or self-complacent satisfaction.'[1] A warning that complacency over material progress might be destructive came from the radical, McCarthy. He pointed out that the Chartist movement was weakened because people had hopes of a better society even without the Charter as conditions improved.[2]

The optimistic view of national progress was perhaps crystallised in what has come to be known as the 'Whig interpretation' of history. This entailed the belief that the English nation had traditionally enjoyed certain rights which had been lost, but reclaimed from the seventeenth century onwards. Thus while the ideal of constitutional progress was upheld, it was to some extent turned into an anti-revolutionary doctrine. Revolution had not triumphed in the past since, it was believed, those who had upheld the prerogatives of the monarchy were the true revolutionaries and had tried to drag the constitution into new and untried courses. Whig historians, of whom Hallam and Macaulay are perhaps the most outstanding examples in the nineteenth century, traced the growth of political freedom from the days of the Saxons, through the triumph of Magna Carta to the development of Parliament in the fourteenth and fifteenth centuries. Then, they believed, the Tudors established a despotic government. However, during the struggles of the Stuart period the power of the monarchy was curbed and English freedom at last regained. This view obtained great currency in the nineteenth century, and indeed before, stemming partly as it does from the writings of John Locke. Lord Chesterfield's advice to his son contains a summary of English history which is in essence the Whig view.[3] Traces of it are to be found in the work of conservative writers such as Hannah More, who describes how Magna Carta, 'that famous deed, without any violent innovation became the mound of property, the pledge of liberty and the guarantee of independence'.[4] Only rarely did signs of opposition to this view appear. Hume's generally dispassionate account of constitutional struggles set him apart from the other great historians whose works were consulted by writers of school textbooks in the nineteenth century. Otherwise it is possible to come across the occasional writer who asserted that 'The liberties of English men are not to be founded on precedent.'[5]

---

[1] Tout (1890), p. 245.
[2] McCarthy, *England after the Reform Bill*, (1899), p. 121.
[3] *Letters from a Nobleman to his Son*, p. 239.
[4] More's *Hints* (1805), p. 174.
[5] *Systematic Education*, by Shepherd, Joyce and Carpenter (1815), p. 284.

Also, though radicals did not dispute the idea of constitutional progress, they could not accept the complacency with which contemporaries were prone to regard the present state of government in England. Cobbett, for instance, wrote: 'This nation, once the greatest and most moral in the world, is now a nation of incorrigible thieves; and in either case the most impoverished, the most fallen, the most degraded that ever saw the light of day.'[1]

As one might expect the Whig interpretation of the nation's constitutional advance is the one accepted in most history textbooks of the period 1800–1914. The Kings of England were in many cases portrayed as constitutional innovators, while those opposed to them were shown to be conservatives, fighting to preserve traditional freedoms. The general attitude of most writers was summed up quite early in the century by Baldwin when he wrote about the proceedings of 1688 and James II's subsequent flight:[2] 'England had been free under the Saxons, the Normans and the Plantagenets; but the sort of freedom enjoyed was not exactly the sort of freedom required in a present state of civilisation; all ideas of regular government had been superseded by the Wars of York and Lancaster. The Tudors had reigned in many respects arbitrarily: the whole period of the Stuarts was a contention between power and liberty and this contention was not entirely closed but by the proceedings of the "Glorious Revolution".' Baldwin had earlier prefaced his remarks by claiming bluntly: 'The Revolution constitutes the final settlement of the government of England.' Besides showing the influence of the 'Whig interpretation', therefore, he also demonstrates another feature of the work of many writers—namely, that he regards the constitution as it existed in his own day as perfect and unlikely to be changed except for the worse.

Opinions about Magna Carta also reveal the way in which the writers of textbooks regarded the progress of constitutional change. The same phrases recur constantly: 'The foundation of our liberties' for instance is found in Gill,[3] Hort,[3] Keightley,[3] Clough,[3] Cooper[3] and Farr[3] with variants such as 'groundwork of English freedom',[4] and 'bulwark of English freedom'.[5] However, Magna Carta is not allowed to appear as a revolutionary docu-

---

[1] Cobbett (1824), p. 477.
[2] Baldwin (1812), pp. 124–5.
[3] Gill (1870), p. 19; Hort (1822), p. 2; Keightley (1841), p. 55; Clough (1870), p. 33; Cooper (1830), p. 20; Farr (1856), p. 131.
[4] Livesey (1908), p. 52.
[5] Ransome (1890), p. 45.

ment, for several writers suggested that English freedom was already established in 1216,[1] and could be traced back even farther: 'Our mode of government is now almost the same as it was in Anglo-Saxon times.'[2] Admittedly other views were expressed about the significance of Magna Carta. Mrs Markham asserted that: 'It rescued our ancestors from much of the oppressive tyranny of the feudal system, and the supreme happiness we enjoy as a nation over the rest of Europe we owe principally to the sense and virtues of those who raised the invaluable bulwark of English history.'[3] She stressed its influence on the present, a feature also notable in later writers.[4]

Indeed the development of Parliament in the Middle Ages was linked by some writers with British freedom in the nineteenth century. Simon de Montfort's career was high in favour, especially towards the end of the period. One author described him as representing 'the great principle of English political life',[5] and another suggested that as a result of his victory at Lewes 'the ultimate control of the government was, in accordance with the Earl's principles, given to the nation'.[6] Repeatedly Parliament was credited with 'privileges very little short of those enjoyed by a modern Parliament'.[7] An elementary school reader of the 1880s claimed that it had been accepted as 'the Representative of the National Will',[8] for nearly four centuries. Such views are not confined to the later part of the century. Baldwin saw the Tudor period as one in which the natural development of the constitution towards liberty was threatened by a series of despotic rulers.[9] He wrote: 'Henry VIII governed the country, once so free, and which afterward conquered her liberties back again, like a Turkish Sultan.' This view of the Tudors as 'hereditary dictators'[10] is a common one. It is combined with the attitude that their Parliaments were 'the unresisting instrument of whatever oppression a ferocious tyrant could devise for gratifying his cruelty, his lust or his caprice'.[11]

There were very few dissentients to the attitudes to constitutional

---

[1] Pinnock (1822), p. 36
[2] *Jack* (1905), vol. 3, p. 241.
[3] Markham (1874), p. 103.
[4] Ransome (1903), p. 87.
[5] Airy (1898), p. 81.
[6] Edwards (1901), p. 767.
[7] Fearenside (1911), p. 1.
[8] *Cassells* (1884), *Class History of England*, p. 274.
[9] Baldwin (1812), p. 91.
[10] Ransome (1890), p. 121.
[11] Curtis (1875), p. 85.

development in the Middle Ages quoted above. The editor of the 1875 edition of Hume's history was at pains to explain to the reader that the author had been mistaken in attributing to the Plantagenets and Tudors powers greater 'than the facts will justify'[1] and admitted that he has endeavoured to put this right. Occasionally Henry VIII's severities were justified on grounds of national emergency.[2] The only writer to adopt a point of view wholly at variance with the 'Whig interpretation' was Bishop Davys who attacked even Magna Carta on the grounds that 'when there is a turbulent and wicked spirit abroad, it is not signing charters that will restore order and happiness'.[3] Moreover, he is unusual in that he expressed the view, generally current in the eighteenth century, that the ideal of balance of the forces within the constitution is the best to aim at. He wrote of Henry VIII's Parliament: 'This is the best of all forms of government and it continues in England to this day. . . . By this form of government, the good of all ranks is consulted, and, if either the king or the lords or the people should attempt to exceed the limits of the power assigned to them, the others are ready to see that all things are properly balanced.'[4] This is a far cry from the unqualified admiration for Parliament which nearly all the other writers expressed.

Again opinions about the struggles between King and Parliament in the seventeenth century were, on the whole, well disposed to the latter. Most authors depicted the Royalists as the revolutionaries or at least as those who were too short-sighted to understand the real meaning of the constitution.

A typical judgment of the reign of Charles I is that: 'The struggle in this reign was between absolute and constitutional monarchy. And the latter prevailed.'[5] In fact the term 'constitutional' was never used until the eighteenth century in such a context. It is used here and elsewhere, even with reference to the reign of Richard II in one book,[6] to suggest that any king who acted without reference to the views of Parliament was acting illegally. Moreover Charles's opponents were seen not as revolutionaries but as conservatives. Hampden, for instance, was typically described in the students' Hume: 'At last in 1637 John Hampden acquired by his spirit and

---

[1] Hume (1875), p. iv.
[2] Morris (1871), p. 218.
[3] Davys (1822), p. 46.
[4] Ibid. pp. 52–3.
[5] *Tower* (1911), vol 4, p. 163.
[6] *Chambers* (1885), p. 82.

courage, universal popularity throughout the nation and his merited great renown with posterity, for the bold stand which he made in defence of the laws and liberties of his country.'[1] In contrast Charles I was depicted as failing to understand his true position: 'The mistake he made was that he thought himself above the laws, and that his subjects were made for the king. . . .'[2] The history of his reign was described as one of 'illegal exactions and repressions'[3] and authors commented on his 'blind obstinacy' in refusing to face the truth of his opponents' arguments.[4]

It is perhaps some evidence of anti-revolutionary feeling that many books tended to gloss over the Civil War, minimising the violence entailed, but uniting to deplore the death of the King. Miss Rodwell expressed an extreme view: 'This wicked and unjust act will always be a sad stain on the history of England',[5] but there was general agreement that the execution was illegal—'Such an act was strange in England; men feared for the peace and liberty of their country',[6]—and that it caused a revulsion of sympathy in favour of the King: 'Feelings of bitterness gave place to commiseration, pity and even admiration.'[7] Nevertheless, some writers could not help remarking that Charles was not wholly blameless. The author of the *History of England Mostly in Words of One Syllable* remarked: 'There is no doubt that he had done much that was most wrong' before adding: 'but his death was more than less a crime, and one for which those who caused it were soon to pay.'[8] Another writer commented that if his conduct had been such as it was at his execution, he would probably have escaped disaster.[9]

Cromwell, as the architect of Charles's execution, gets on the whole a favourable reception from the textbooks, however. He was sometimes shown as the champion of law and order[10] who 'curbed the violence of faction; bestowed the benefits of religious toleration upon all religious sects but the popish; and administered justice with strict impartiality', and as 'a brave, skilful soldier, a bold, wise and successful ruler, and one of the most

---

[1] Hume (1875), p. 391.
[2] *Blackwoods* (1883), vol.III, p. 40.
[3] Farr (1856), p. 289.
[4] Conan and Kendall (1902), p. 271.
[5] Rodwell (1844), p. 161.
[6] Edwards (1901), p. 156.
[7] Farr (1856), p. 289.
[8] (1907), p. 63.
[9] Littlewood (1869), p. 94.
[10] Hort (1822), p. 3.

wonderful men in history'.[1] It is true that Cromwell was criticised for his oppression[2] and his ambition.[3] On the whole the majority of writers admired the Protector, however. Partly this may be due to his successful wars abroad and to the efforts of Carlyle in publicising his achievement. However, these explanations do not fit the anti-nationalist writers whose work dates from early in the century, e.g. Hort and Baldwin. Possibly Cromwell's popularity may be ascribed to the fact that he appeared to be the champion of Protestantism against the papal leanings of the Stuarts and the defender of the liberty and the constitution of England against attacks from the same quarter. His revolutionary aspects were played down.

The same is true of the Revolution of 1688. In this connection James II was generally seen as 'one of the most intolerable sovereigns that ever reigned over a free people'.[4] He was attacked both for his attempts to restore Roman Catholicism and for his 'unconstitutional' behaviour. The general view of the events of 1688 was that they saved England in two ways: 'The Revolution not only lessened the power of the Crown, but it was the death-blow to the hopes of the Catholics in England.'[5] Some writers saw the Revolution as setting the final seal on Parliament's claim to be the traditional centre of power in the constitution: 'William and Mary were set upon the throne by Parliament and since that time no one has been able to pretend that the Kings of England rule except by Parliament.'[6]

There were, however, a minority of dissenting views to the 'Whig interpretation' of the constitutional struggles in the seventeenth century. One author saw the Parliamentarians as revolutionaries: 'They were no friends to public liberty; for never under the most arbitrary monarch were the people of England subject to a more rigid tyranny. . . . But it is ever so in revolutions. A few violent men take the lead; their voice and their activity seem to multiply their numbers; the great body of the people either indolent or pusillanimous are led in triumph at the chariot wheels of paltry faction.'[7] Another author who shared this opinion saw the lesson of the Civil War as: 'It will not be more christian than politically wise in the end to endure oppression rather than resist it with illegitimate weapons.'[8]

---

[1] Bullock (1861), p. 160.
[2] Cooper (1848), p. 67.
[3] Pinnock (1822), p. 51.
[4] Cooper (1830), p. 87.
[5] *Holborn* (1882), Book 2, p. 146.
[6] Ransome (1905), p. 264.
[7] Gleig (1853), p. 36.
[8] Milner (1852), p. 579.

It is perhaps no mere chance that these two writers published their books for 'The Society for Promoting Christian Knowledge' and 'The Religious Tract Society' respectively. Another book in which the Whig view was refuted was written by Father Flanagan. In his catechism we read: 'Question: When Charles I had continued yielding to their wishes, until the House of Commons had become more powerful than it had ever been before, did he not at last refuse to do anything more for it? Answer: Yes. Question: What followed? Answer: Civil War.'[1] A fellow Roman Catholic historian, Livesey, also took a somewhat pro-Royalist stand, though he was much more moderate than Flanagan. He referred to Charles's 'duplicity'[2] and suggested that his opponents genuinely cared for liberty. Although the Whig view of the constitutional struggles of the past did on the whole prevail, therefore, the opposing Tory view did not die out completely, especially in Anglican and Roman Catholic circles.

Whatever their point of view, however, few writers assumed that progress towards political liberty must necessarily lead to the growth of democracy. Writing in 1828, Macaulay, in a review of Hallam's history, was somewhat guarded in his views on Parliamentary reform which he believed should be undertaken to prevent the worse perils of a revolution. He wrote: 'It will soon be necessary to reform that we may preserve, to save the fundamental principles of the Constitution by alteration in the subordinate parts. It will then be possible, as it was possible two hundred years ago, to protect vested rights, to secure every useful institution endeared by antiquity and noble associations, and at the same time, to introduce into the system improvements harmonising with the original plan.'[3] The radical disturbances which followed the Napoleonic wars, the Chartist agitations of the middle of the century, and the continuance of agitation for manhood suffrage and far-reaching social and political reforms which continued outside Parliament throughout the century, serve to explain the fear of democracy which affected the upper and middle classes, many of whom had been reared on the Whig interpretation of the constitution. As Dicey pointed out, both radical reformers and conservatives were united in the delusion that manhood suffrage would inevitably result in the violent and far-reaching changes demanded by the former.[4] Hence fear of revolution on the pattern of France in 1789 was coupled with fear

---

[1] Flanagan *(c.* 1850), p. 45.
[2] Livesey (1908), p. 20.
[3] *Essays* (1907 ed.), p. 75.
[4] *Law and Opinion* (1905), p. 57.

of democracy. Writers throughout the century repeated the argument that education of the masses was the only means of stopping the activities of the revolutionary and the demagogue. In a pamphlet entitled *Observations on the Causes of Failure in Education for the Subordinate Classes of Society* the writer complained that the lower classes were not receiving an education which would enable them to withstand such pernicious influences as the popular Press.[1] Brougham's *Society for the Propagation of Useful Knowledge* was an attempt to remedy this defect. However, the complaints continued until the Education Act of 1870. Thereafter discussion centred more on the exact means by which the pupil could be trained in good citizenship. E. E. Morris, speaking on the teaching of history in 1875, suggested that: 'If one object in education be the formation of good citizens—and no one will deny that this is one object, even if he would not allow it the paramount importance which I should—then it is impossible to omit from education that branch of knowledge which is concerned with the duties of citizens, or the training in the attainment of that kind of knowledge.'[2] Morris went on to assert that he did not envisage history to be used for the purposes of any one party, nor does he express contempt or fear for the newly enfranchised classes. However, such feelings were to be found in academic circles up to the outbreak of the First World War. Frank J. Adkins wrote in *History*: 'I need not dwell upon the importance of history teaching in these days of triumphant democracy, and until we get the universal evening school it is the only place our masters can get any training in.'[3] On the whole, however, fear of revolution or far-reaching reform had faded by the early years of this century. Party animosities were no longer expressed in such bitter terms. Dicey pointed out that if the old upholders of the constitution of the eighteenth century as perfect and immutable had died away so had those who would have overturned it completely. England was full of 'the ghosts of dead ideals' and in their place political controversy had become less embittered, more polite and more practical'.[4]

Echoes of the suspicions of democracy can be detected in opinions expressed in many history textbooks about the 1832 and other Reform Bills. Even those writers whose books were published in the middle of the century were not on the whole certain that the changes of 1832 were wise. One author noted that it seemed to many at that time that the constitution could

---

[1] (1826), p. 13.
[2] Reported in the *Educational Times* (1 Feb. 1875), p. 249.
[3] *History* (1912), vol. I, p. 20.
[4] *Law and Opinion* (1905), p. 440.

only change for the worse.[1] He also bitterly attacked the 'wild schemes' put forward then and lamented that their supporters included even those 'who had begun their public life as Tories'. Another writer of the same period asserted: 'It still remains a doubt whether the measure was worth the price it cost; namely a disruption of friendship, the loss of life and property, and the agitation of the whole kingdom.'[2] However, from the mid-century onwards opinions began to change. Farr, who was apparently more liberal in his views than Scott whose work he revised, remarked in a work which he wrote himself: 'That which was deemed a curse has proved a blessing',[3] and such judgments as that the people in 1832 had 'now at length gained possession of the legislature which had long pretended falsely to represent them'[4] became increasingly common. Towards the end of the century the 1832 Act had come to seem 'a very moderate and necessary measure of reform'.[5] Even the 1867 Bill was praised because it enfranchised 'many intelligent Englishmen' who had been left without votes in 1832.[6]

Nevertheless the writers of school textbooks took good care to stress that there was nothing revolutionary in all these changes in the franchise. The author of the *Chambers Reader* asserted that: 'Reform in our country prevents revolution'[7] and there was an attempt on the part of a few authors to suggest that Englishmen were merely regaining their former rights: 'Once upon a time nearly all Englishmen had had the vote. It was high time that this absurd system should be reformed.'[8] Moreover a small group of writers took occasion to stress to their child readers the responsibilities and dangers of democracy. For example, one warned: 'I trust, my young friends, when you are older and called upon to make use of the powers which your forefathers never had, both you and the statesman you elect will remember that "wisdom is better than strength" and that "righteousness exalteth a nation",'[9] and another author begged her readers to 'consider very carefully the far-reaching effects of any change which seems to promise a present benefit. Past history teaches those who grasp at too much are likely to lose more than they gain.'[10]

---

[1] Gleig (1853), p. 605.
[1] Scott and Farr (1861), p. 688.
[3] Farr (1856), p. 444.
[4] Bright (1875), p. 1432.
[5] *Raleigh* (1897), vol. 5, p. 33.
[6] *Blackwoods* (1883), vol. 3, p. 224.
[7] *Chambers* (1885), p. 205.
[8] *Warwick* (1896), vol. 5, p. 160.
[9] Gill (1870), p. 72.
[10] Buckley (1904), p. 148.

The distaste for all things revolutionary can be clearly seen in the opinions of the writers with regard to the revolts and civil disturbances of the past. In this context, it is interesting to compare the treatment of the Peasant's Revolt of 1381 with that of more recent risings. In the main there was considerable sympathy for the peasants, and astonishingly little stress on their violence, especially when we consider that in fact the Treasurer and the Archbishop of Canterbury were among the victims of the revolt and that a good deal of property was destroyed in it.[1] It is true that some authors stressed Tyler's insolence and lack of manners and commented on the 'innumerable disorders'.[2] Pitt, whose *History of England with the Wars left out* is really a tirade against war and violence of any kind, exclaimed in horror that not only was Tyler a rebel, but he 'destroyed public buildings'.[3] For the most part, however, every excuse was made for the peasants. 'Little Arthur' was told by Lady Callcott that Tyler was 'a bold brave man wishing to do right',[4] and the author of the *Chambers Reader* excused the peasants on the grounds that 'as was natural with men who had long been cruelly treated, they committed many acts of violence'.[5] Other writers depicted Tyler as a 'humble patriot',[6] pointed out the unfairness of the poll tax imposed and the 'brutality' of the tax-collector,[7] and stressed that the peasants were 'grossly ill-treated'.[8] Another writer went so far as to depict the rebels as 'socialists' and adds that they 'were looked upon as more dangerous than they really were. They wanted to abolish serfdom which was right. They also wanted to lay hands on the revenues of the Church; this naturally aroused the fears of all who had property.'[9] In dealing with the actual events of the rising and its suppression the writers also show considerable sympathy for the rebels. The author of the *Chambers New Scheme Reader* asserts that 'on the whole they were better behaved and more orderly than might be expected'[10] and Miss Corner declared that their demands were 'not unreasonable'.[11] Others

---

[1] See above, p. 35.
[2] Cooper (1830), p. 35.
[3] Pitt (1893), p. 34.
[4] Callcott (1872), p. 103.
[5] Chambers (1885), p. 82.
[6] Collins (1890), p. 81.
[7] Edwards (1901), p. 117.
[8] Farr (1856), p. 72.
[9] Pringle (1907), p. 43.
[10] *Chambers* (1901), vol. 3, p. 46.
[11] *Corner* (1885), p. 113.

described Richard's 'treachery'.[1] and how he 'breaks all his promises and compels the peasantry to return to slavery'.[2]

Many writers took a less tolerant view of the more recent disturbances which occurred after the end of the Napoleonic Wars, in a period of grave financial difficulty, especially for the poor. The cause of the unrest was commonly attributed to 'the instigation of Hunt'[3] in the case of Peterloo, and the latter was often dubbed a 'notorious mob orator'[4] or, more commonly, 'a demagogue'.[5] Likewise the rising at Spafields was ascribed to the 'inflammatory harangues of some political enthusiasts'.[6] The disturbances themselves were described variously as 'scenes of violence and retribution',[7] 'a considerable political agitation'[8] or 'seditious assemblies'.[9] An extreme example of a hostile account of the Peterloo meeting is provided by Kipling and Fletcher who stated bluntly: 'At one riot in Manchester in 1819 the soldiers had to be called in and several people were shot.'[10] The anti-radical tone of this passage can be clearly seen from the way in which the word 'riot' is used to describe the gathering, and it is suggested that the army 'had' to be called in, i.e. because the people were dangerous. Moreover the account is inaccurate since most of the victims were not shot but trampled under foot in the effort to escape from the sabres of the yeomanry, or wounded by the latter. Kipling and Fletcher went on to add that some people complained because innocent people might have been killed, noting in reply: 'Those who get up riots are usually careful to keep out of the way when the suppression begins.' Several other writers also gave accounts of Peterloo which stressed the danger of the situation and justified the decision to call out the troops. Mrs Markham, writing near to the event, described the crowd as 'a mob of at least 8,000 people'. She suggested that the troops were called out because there were fears of a riot and added, almost as an afterthought, that they 'in doing so had the misfortune to kill four persons and wound forty more'.[11] A later author asserted that the meeting assembled 'with some form of military discipline'.[12]

---

[1] Conan and Kendall (1902), p. 141.
[2] Grimaldi (1871), p. 102.
[3] Beale (1858), p. 136.
[4] White (1860), p. 757.
[5] Hume (1875), p. 706.
[6] Cooper (1830), p. 188.
[7] Ibid.
[8] Curtis (1875), p. 145.
[9] Farr (1856), p. 654.
[10] Fletcher and Kipling (1911), p. 225.
[11] Markham (1874), p. 471.
[12] Tout (1890), p. 1481.

The Cato Street conspiracy was also treated in such a way that it became a piece of anti-radical propaganda. It was variously described as 'a most atrocious plot to assassinate the king's ministers and burn London'[1] and a 'daringly atrocious plot'.[2] No mention was made of the facts, perhaps unknown to the writers, that Thistlewood was of unsound mind and that the whole plot was organised largely at the instigation of a government spy. One author even saw the failure of the plot as a sign of divine concern for the Tory government of the day. 'But there is a controlling power which seldom permits plans so hideous to be accomplished.'[3] It is a feature of many of the textbooks examined that they often did not mention any of the disturbances of the period 1815–20 in detail and when they singled one out for mention, it was often Cato Street, in many ways the least typical of them all. For instance, Murby, a book with a very wide sale, comes into this category.

Nevertheless, there are a substantial number of writers who took a more favourable view of the activities of the radicals and criticised the government of the day for its attitude towards them. Most of these date from the later years of the nineteenth century or the early years of the twentieth, though one critic of the authorities' behaviour at Peterloo was a contemporary.[4]

Some writers attributed disturbances to 'heavy taxation and the high price of food'[5] and the author of one elementary school reader commented of the Cato Street conspiracy that it 'shows how desperate bad government and bad social conditions had made some of the people'.[6] Moreover the government's handling of the disturbances in general was criticised: 'The government, fearful lest the people should get the upper hand as they had done in France, used force to keep them quiet instead of trying to cure their grievances.'[7] The circumstances of the Peterloo incident occasionally called forth anger. One author referred to its 'sheer mismangagement'[8] and another to the 'incapacity of the Tory party', adding: 'As usual in England the employment of the military except in the very last necessity excited the anger of very many, even of the wealthier classes.'[9] Elsewhere it was

---

1 *Collins* (1890), p. 220.
2 Ross (1873), p. 58.
3 Gleig (1856), p. 604.
4 Cooper (1830), p. 197.
5 Pringle (1907), p. 20.
6 *Tower* (1911), vol. 7, p. 20.
7 Ransome (1905), p. 364.
8 Airy (1898), p. 454.
9 Bright (1875), p. 1353.

asserted that the magistrates acted 'rashly and cruelly'[1] bringing about 'unprovoked slaughter',[2] so that 'even women were cut down by the ungallant sabres of the military'.[3] One writer held that the incident caused many people to 'take up the cause of Parliamentary reform'.[4] There was also hostility on the part of many writers to the Six Acts which followed Peterloo. It is true that one author regarded them as 'called for by the state of the country', though he also describes them as 'decidedly coercive'.[5] Elsewhere they were referred to as 'This unjust code of laws'[6] and it was suggested that they were used to hamper the Englishman's right to free speech. On the whole a slight majority of writers do, however, exhibit some signs of animus against the radical side and this is confirmed, perhaps, by the fact that many, even in the latter part of the nineteenth century, did not mention either the radical disturbances or the Six Acts.

The Chartists were more harshly regarded than their counterparts at the beginning of the century, perhaps because they are so much nearer in time to the majority of the writers who mention them. Lady Callcott, for instance, described them as ruled by some 'designing persons' and alleged that they 'thought this would be a good time to try and frighten the Queen and government into granting their foolish and dangerous wishes. . . . But the people of England loved the Queen too well, and were too well satisfied with the government of their country to let the Chartists do any mischief.'[7] Elsewhere they were referred to as 'discontented people'[8] or 'lawless men'[9] and even the mildest of their protests was greeted with horror: 'Another of their practices was to go in procession to the churches and to take possession of the body of the edifice; a few among them have even been known to smoke their pipes and keep on their hats, as if in defiance of the customary reverential deportment.'[10] One lady author claimed that they used so much violence that law-abiding people were in constant dread of them.[11] The stress on the violent and decluded nature of the Chartists is widespread in those authors who mention them and even

---

[1] Carter (1911), p. 164.
[2] Bullock (1861), p. 228.
[3] Ross (1872), p. 50.
[4] Morris (1883), p. 464.
[5] Mauder (1864), p. 479.
[6] *Jack* (1905), vol. 3, p. 108.
[7] Callcott (1872), p. 261.
[8] Corner (1885), p. 295.
[9] Ibid. p. 301.
[10] Farr (1856), p. 452.
[11] Ransome (1903), p. 382.

one who denied that they were really dangerous to law and order added: 'But it is rightly held to be unconstitutional to threaten Parliament with even the appearance of force.'[1]

There remains, however, a noticeable minority of writers who took a moderate and even approving attitude towards the Chartists. Some, for instance, admitted there was a difference between 'physical force Chartism' and the peaceful branch of the movement.[2] The Irish radical, Justin McCarthy, went even further and suggested that the future lay with the supporters of the Chartist movement: 'It would be to mis-read the teachings of history, if we were to suppose that any popular clause with a real grievance behind it could be suppressed in a country such as England by mere persecutions and sentences of transportation.'[3] Other writers after the passing of the 1884 Reform Bill described the Chartist demands as 'not so unreasonable after all'[4] and one even admitted: 'Though most of the six points (the Chartist demands) have been gained, the social ills which the Chartists desired to amend are still existing.'[5] There is some evidence that the animus against the Chartists lessened as the nineteenth century wore on, therefore, and, as in the case of the radical unrest in the period 1815-20, there is scarcely much difference in the treatment between the books intended for colleges and public schools and the readers designed for use in voluntary and state-aided education. On the other hand, it is perhaps worth remarking that very few of the latter mention the Chartists in any detail.

The French Revolution, in contrast, provides an interesting example of a subject whose treatment, unlike those of the radical unrest and the Chartists, actually become less moderate as the century wore on. The continuator of Dodsley's history, by implication mocked those who hated the revolution and did their best to stamp out those who sympathised with it in England: 'But he that is foolish and obstinate, that plotteth mischief against his king and country, to kindle the flames of war in our bosoms, let Botany Bay be his dwelling place and the New Drop his portion.'[6] A less expected sympathiser with the Revolution, at least in its beginnings, is Baldwin. He admitted that 'unhappily the French nation went about their

---

[1] Morris (1882), vol. 3, p. 242.
[2] Knight (1865), p. 911.
[3] McCarthy, *England after the Reform Bill* (1899), pp. 114-15.
[4] Conan and Kendall (1901), p. 405.
[5] Hassall (1901), p. 545.
[6] Dodsley (1796), p. 154.

undertaking too eagerly',[1] yet he added: 'As they are a refined and polished people their neighbours at first sympathised with their efforts.' Baldwin's moderate attitude does not seem to have done him harm in the eyes of his countrymen, for his publisher was able to quote a review taken from the *Monthly Review* 1806, which commented: 'The bias of the writer is of that sort with which we should least quarrel, since it is in favour of the rights of the subject.' Moreover, although one early writer noted that: 'For some time a set of wicked and disaffected persons in France had projected a revolution',[2] a more typical view seems to have been that Englishmen supported the Revolution on the whole until it began to result in wholesale bloodshed. 'At its commencement no true Briton could avoid rejoicing to see a great and numerous people breaking the chains of tyranny, and springing forward to light and freedom. But as it proceeded, such sanguinary scenes arose to view as excited abhorrence.'[3]

By the middle of the century, however, opinions about the French Revolution were harsher. A typical view was that: 'A terrible revolution broke out in France which plunged the continent of Europe into deepest gloom . . . by which nations were shaken to their foundations, thrones overturned, and fertile districts drenched in blood',[4] and great stress was laid on the innocence of Louis XVI.[5] One of the most highly coloured accounts of the Terror in France comes from Ross, though since, as we know, he was of a radical turn of mind, there is the usual doubt as to whether he was really serious. He recounted how 'crunch went the knife on the beautiful Marie-Antoinette', and then described 'the glorious ringlets heavy with gore-gouts, the sweet lips pale'. The death of Louis was made the excuse for the following hyperbole: '. . . But when the head of Louis fell with a dull thud upon the scaffold, Europe awoke with a shriek from her reverie of horror'.[6] Although such opinions about the Revolution persisted up until 1914, there are a few indications of a less emotional approach. The author of *Tower Readers*, for instance, commented favourably on the fact that although very disruptive in its effects, 'everywhere it gave a wider horizon to men's eyes and nobler aspiration to their hearts, although at first it was disgraced by innumerable horrors.'[7]

---

[1] Baldwin (1812), p. 140.
[2] Trimmer (1849), p. 308.
[3] Hort (1822), p. 203.
[4] Clough (1870), p. 85.
[5] Keightley (1841), p. 333.
[6] Ross (1872), p. 23.
[7] *Tower* (1911), vol. 7, p. 85.

The influence of the more tranquil political atmosphere in England by the later years of the nineteenth century is more marked in the attitudes of the writers to politicians and statesmen of their own time. On the whole, authors of textbooks were much criticised for neglecting recent history, so examples on this topic are somewhat difficult to come by. As a general rule, however, it appears that as the century progressed, writers were much milder in their attitudes and careful to express their opinions in moderate terms. At first, for instance, there were really violent attacks on Castlereagh whose suicide is described: 'Though the event was melancholy in itself, it proved a great benefit to the nation. His lordship seems to have aimed at the annihilation of public liberty.'[1] Wellington was depicted in his own lifetime as 'the betrayer of his sovereign and his country'[2] for his part in passing Catholic Emancipation and soon after his death Bright wrote of his part in the events of 1832: 'His conduct as head of the government was so peculiar that it would scarcely have been tolerated in a less influential man. . . . He fought till his opponents became irresistible and then suddenly retreated, without thinking it necessary to resign office on account of his defeat.'[3] The praise of Wellington by his admirers sounds rather tame, though Lady Maria Callcott dubs him 'the greatest general of our time'.[4]

In contrast the supporters of Mr Gladstone and Mr Disraeli conducted their battles in muted tones. The author of the *Collins Reader* commented on the latter's 'great abilities'[5] and in the *Jack Readers* he was described as a 'gifted Jew'.[6] Another writer stressed the 'moderate and judicious concessions' by which he managed to carry the Reform Bill of 1867.[7] Elsewhere Disraeli was criticised for his abandonment of Protection and his subsequent failure in debate: 'But unpractised in finance, he gave an easy opening to the greatest master of the subject, Mr Gladstone.'[8] However the latter did not entirely escape censure. His Home Rule Bill was criticised for seemingly 'leading to the disintegration of the Empire'.[9] On the whole, however, his work was favourably received. Other writers attributed

---

[1] Cooper (1830), p. 209.
[2] Cooper (1843), p. 167.
[3] Bright (1875), p. 1401.
[4] Callcott (1875), p. 250.
[5] *Collins* (1890), p. 232.
[6] *Jack* (1905), p. 220.
[7] Murby (1895). p. 170.
[8] Airy (1898), p. 488.
[9] Hassall (1901), p. 581.

to Gladstone and the Liberal party the fact that: 'Britain is today one of the most democratic countries in Europe.'[1]

It is perhaps relevant here to note that although personalities are sometimes attacked, parties go on the whole unmentioned. It is true that the author of the *Warwick Readers* attacked Oxford University as 'a stronghold of Toryism and intolerance'[2] as if the two went automatically together, but most writers would, it seems, have been willing to accept the view of Ransome, one of the very few authors to attempt to explain the basis of party politics in his own day. 'Liberalism has at bottom the idea of progress and conservatism that of stability and the world can no more dispense with one than with the other. Each needs the other, and the more a state is regulated in accordance with the needs of both, the more fitted is it to supply the wants of the people with whose welfare it is charged.'[3] Those who wanted different and greater changes in society than the Liberal party were largely ignored. As we have seen, the peasants of 1381 were compared, not too harshly, with socialists and we get the same impression of the latter being relatively harmless, but impractical and deluded, from a writer who described Owen's 'wild scheme of Socialism'.[4] One or two authors were at pains to distinguish the dangerous radicals of the beginning of the nineteenth century from those of the same name who were to be found on the right wing of the Liberal party, by its end. The author of *Historical Reasons Why* explained: 'The name of Radical in its early adoption was used by the more moderate as a term of reproach, signifying a noisy and unreasonable demagogue—a party whose existence was a symbol of anarchy and strife. At the present day, however, the word possesses a very different connotation.'[5]

In general, it is a marked feature of political opinions in school textbooks that they mirror those of society at large so quickly and so completely. The tolerance of the enlightenment still existed at the beginning of the nineteenth century and may account for moderate references to the French Revolution which date from that period. The succeeding generation of writers felt with particular intensity a fear of revolutionary activity which showed itself in England in radical and Chartist disturbances, but by the end of the century this fear and the bitterness of party strife were on the

---

[1] Conan and Kendall (1901), p. 412.
[2] *Warwick* (1896), vol. 7, p. 192.
[3] Ransome (1890), p. 226.
[4] Tout (1890), p. 242.
[5] *Historical Reason Why* (1859), p. 290.

[65]

wane and more balanced opinions reappeared. Even at the time of greatest anti-revolutionary feeling among the middle and upper classes of society, however, there are glimpses of sympathy for the unfortunate of a distant era, such as the peasants of 1381, which suggest that there was no concerted or thoroughgoing desire to make history textbooks into a form of anti-revolutionary propaganda. Nor is there any significance difference in the treatment of controversial political topics in books intended for fee-paying independent and state elementary schools.

Similarly the general acceptance of the Whig interpretation of history can be seen as evidence of complacency about the constitutional development of England, but it is really more realistic to regard it as evidence of acceptance of a set of opinions widely, indeed almost uniformly, held among academic and literary historians of the nineteenth century. It offers no real evidence of a conscious effort to preach quietism to the rising generation. Only with regard to the monarchy does there seem to have been anything like a conspiracy of silence about republican activity. Certainly although this was widespread, and not only among the working class, it is not surprising that writers chose to omit reference to a controversy which centres on the key-stone of the British constitution. But even here it is possible to interpret this as evidence of a set of moral rather than political opinions. Approval of a particular monarch was generally made dependent on moral worth in the history textbooks and since the throne was occupied by monarchs of high moral repute for the greater part of the period 1800–1914 it is not surprising that references to them were complimentary. As we shall see in the next chapter, those monarchs who transgressed against current notions of respectability or morality were certainly not immune from criticism.

CHAPTER III

Opinions about Morality

'Ignorance is the foul parent of vice; and vice leads to
every infraction of the laws, which are sanctioned for
the protection of the life and property of others.'[1]

I N Victorian England morality and national stability traditionally went
hand in hand. One result of this was that the desire to inculcate virtue
through education was found in public and elementary school alike. It
would certainly be wrong to assume that the upper ranks of society wished
to foist on the children of the working class a moral code which they did
not consider it important to teach their own. A. H. Layard, speaking on
'The influence of education upon national character' commended the
influence of independent schools and remarked: 'It is the want of this
proper training of the mind, and of this earnest thought-breeding sincerity,
truthfulness and self-reliance which we may have to deplore in modern
state education and its effects on the national character.'[2] History was often
considered to be 'the nursery of patriotism and public virtue'[3] and certainly
the modern reader may be struck by the appearance of a rigid and apparently unvarying set of ethical standards which are displayed in many textbooks of the period 1800–1914. These were naturally those of the respectable middle class to which most of the authors belonged. Behind this
façade of dogmatic certainty, however, there lay various points of controversy. Not only was there no general agreement as to the efficacy of history
as a moral tutor, but in several respects the moral code presented actually
changed with succeeding generations.

During the nineteenth century there was widespread support for the
view that history was a source of moral examples, good and bad. A writer
in the *Nithesay Miscellany* declared that it showed 'examples of all that
is magnanimous, as well as all that is vile; of all that debases and all that
enobles mankind'.[4] Some disputed that it could show many instances of

---

[1] *Educational Times* (October 1854), p. 202.
[2] In *Aberdeen Rectorial Addresses* (1902), p. 83.
[3] *Educational Times* (May 1887), p. 137. Report of a lecture, by H. C. Bowen.
[4] 1812, p. 341.
[5] *Philosophy of Education* (1836), p. 146.

virtuous conduct. For James Simpson it was merely A CHRONICLE OF ANIMAL PROPENSITIES, showing the 'chaos of selfishness which engulfs mankind'.[1] One author of a textbook with clear evangelical leanings declared it 'a cruel thing to put the history of our own country into the hands of children' and gave a catalogue of the vicious acts which it contained, adding that 'an antidote against the poison' must be added in the form of comments on moral principles from the author.[1] Most writers took a more balanced view, however, and there was some feeling that history allowed all pupils to achieve a vicarious experience of the world which would enable them to avoid its dangers when they met them in reality. Chapman most clearly and forcibly expressed this view when he wrote: 'As it is better to learn wisdom from the fate of others who have lived before us, then to trust our own experience and confirmed observation of what passes round us, History is recommended to youth as the parent of knowledge and the great instructress of human life. In history we survey the various generations of mankind passing, as it were, in review before our eyes. There we observe the different characters of men and mark their fate, discern their superior advantages of wisdom and virtue, and learn that misfortune and shame are the natural portion of folly and vice.'[2] Such views were expressed late into the century. A writer in the *National Schoolmaster* began by quoting a recent remark by the Bishop of Manchester to the effect that 'The scholars of our Sunday schools supply the brothels and the gin shops' and blamed this unfortunate state of affairs onto the type of literature which was allowed to pollute the minds of the young. Instead he recommended 'solid intellectual food' and gives as examples of this the crusaders besieging Jerusalem, Elizabeth and the Spanish Armada, the contest between King and Parliament and the French Revolutionary Wars.[3] Even at the beginning of the twentieth century educationists continued to stress the value of history in the formation of good moral conduct. A writer in *History* who criticised over-simplified moral judgments admitted that history did give the child a glimpse into a wider world of experience which would help him to regulate his future conduct.[4]

In contrast, a group of writers throughout the period were not convinced

---

[1] *English History* (1832).
[2] *Essay on Education* (1790), pp. 205–6.
[3] Dec. 1871, p. 28.
[4] 1912, vol. I, p. 34.

that moral judgements should be drawn from history. They are especially to be found among the reviewers who were called upon to read and comment on history textbooks for educational journals. A reviewer in *Transactions of the Education Society* was vehement against the moralising of Dr Ince whom he sarcastically accused of foisting his ideas of morality onto his young readers.[1] Similarly a reviewer in the *Educational Times* advocated a 'plain unvarnished narrative' as preferable to the moral lessons contained in *Henry's First History of England*.[2] Such opinions were even more forcibly expressed at the beginning of the next century. In an article on 'The Seven Deadly Sins of Historical Teaching' Hilda Johnstone named 'moral mongering' as the second[3] and in a later edition of the same periodical J. Headlam protested that 'a conventional presentation of unreal morality can only be false, hypocritical and loathsome'.[4]

Ostensibly there was less disagreement about the virtues which were considered most essential in the nineteenth and early twentieth centuries. William Barrow, writing in a book published at the beginning of the period, listed the good qualities which he hoped to find in his pupils. They included sincerity, honesty, generosity, industry and gratitude.[5] With the addition of chastity this list includes most of the virtues which remained fashionable into the Victorian era. It is notable that charity as such is missing from Barrow's list (unless it be included in generosity). Honesty was particularly admired. The Victorians reacted against what they believed to be the corruption and graft of the previous century. With their widening commercial interests they came to believe that 'honesty was the best policy', as indeed it sometimes was in business. Moreover, it accorded well with the interests of the upper and middle classes to instil the ideal of honesty into the classes who formed their labour force. Hence this question in a catechism of 1856: 'What are honest practices ? was met with the reply : 'Respect to the property and just rights of others, and living on our own means and industry.'[6] Others favoured virtues such as thrift and industry are also connected with the widespread belief in Victorian society that any man could rise in the world by his own hard work and that if he became a pauper and dependent on the parish for relief, it was his own fault.

---

[1] 1854, p. 424.
[2] 1 Oct. 1868, p. 161.
[3] *History* (1912), p. 91.
[4] Ibid. (1918), p. 17.
[5] *Essay on Education* (1802), pp. 219–20.
[6] Quoted in *The Victorians*, edited by Joan Evans (1966), p 79.

When making moral pronouncements writers of the last century tended to concentrate more on a list of vices rather than virtues. Barrow, whose list of virtues has been quoted above, devoted 23 pages to a description of the vices which might be expected in his pupils. They included deceit, selfish meanness, cruelty, sulking, swearing and debauchery.[1] Cruelty in all its forms was especially deplored throughout the nineteenth century and so was the sort of ambition which showed itself in rulers in their love of flattery and desire for conquest. Many writers deplored not only war itself, but the effect of war on those who took part in it. James Simpson lamented the fact that history, as taught up to his own time, had resulted in an admiration of war and plunder,[2] and a governess wrote that history should show conquerors as the idle, boastful brutes which they tended to be.[3] Such views are similar to that expressed by Florence Nightingale during the Crimean War: 'What the horrors of war are no one can imagine. They are not wounds, and blood, and fever, spotted and low, and dysentery, chronic and acute, and cold and heat and famine. They are intoxication, drunken brutality, demoralisation and disorder on the part of the inferior; jealousies, meanness, indifference, selfish brutality on the part of the superior.'[4] Although dislike of war was expressed throughout the nineteenth century and up until the outbreak of the First World War, it does appear that there was less insistence on the moral evils attendant on fighting by the end of the period. Admiration for the courage and qualities of character displayed, for instance, by General Gordon and Baden-Powell suggest that by the turn of the twentieth century the soldier was the hero rather than the villain of society. According to the revised code of 1899 at least twelve of the thirty stories from the period 1688 to the present time intended for study in Standard V were wholly devoted to wars or to war heroes.

In this connection it is relevant to look at the virtues of Alfred, one of the most highly praised of the heroes mentioned in children's history books throughout the nineteenth century. He was commended in many books for his qualities of honesty, modesty, self-effacement and unselfishness. The author of the *Collins Reader* remarked: 'We see a noble and unselfish king, earnestly desiring to live worthily, to do justly and to promote the

---

1 *Essay on Education*, pp. 224–47.
2 *Philosophy of Education* (1836), p. 148.
3 *Experimental Education* (1843), pp. 69–70.
4 Quoted in *The Victorians*, edited by J. Evans (1966), p. 25.

best interests of his people.'[1] Unlike such tyrants as Julius Caesar, who exhibited selfish ambition, Alfred's first consideration was the English people so that he was 'always thinking and working for his people's welfare'.[2] Moreover, he was shown as 'religious before God'[3] and although his military prowess was praised, he was most respected as a man of peace and kindliness: 'As a warrior, his wars were conducted in self-defence and his victories were never stained by cruelty.'[4] The story of the cakes was frequently told and used to illustrate Alfred's modesty and honesty, 'for he was so good that he well knew that it is right to be meek, and to own up when we have done wrong'.[5] Miss Yonge included a poem to Alfred's greatness which touched on some of the virtues of that allegedly modest, gentle and kindly hero, and the influence that it was hoped that he would have:

> 'For his eye afar was set
> Where his soul is resting now,
> And Holy faith was the crown that prest
> *That* steadfast monarch's brow.
> He was England's noblest son
> He is England's comfort styled:
> O well has King Alfred this title won
> From every loyal English child.'[6]

The fact that Alfred's qualities as a war leader were not stressed perhaps indicates the low value which was placed on martial virtues by some authors throughout the nineteenth century. In the introduction to his history one author wrote: 'Let her not enter into the details of sanguinary battles; of crimes which shock humanity and disgrace human nature; let her not display in glaring deceitful colours, the pernicious glories and desolating triumphs of ambition; let her rather record the honourable struggles of our nation in defence of liberty; the advances of useful knowledge; the Progress of Science and Arts, of Agriculture and manufactures. . . . Thus may she afford salutary warning and beneficial instruction.'[7] In general the earlier writers were not prone to over-estimate the

---

1 *Collins* (1890), p. 27.
2 *Cassells* (1883), p. 51.
3 Ibid.
4 Morris (1883), p. 18.
5 Yonge (1880), Book 2, p. 10.
6 Ibid. pp. 61–2.
7 Hort (1822), p. 1.

value of the soldier to the community. Baldwin asked his readers which was the greater man, Cromwell or Milton his secretary, and obviously expected the answer that the man of peace should be valued above the man of war.[1] Mrs Markham stressed the moral responsibilities of the commander.[2] When George tells his mother that he thinks it glorious to die in battle, she severely rebukes him and replies: 'Alas! my child, I fear your dazzled imagination runs away with your judgment. To me there appears something very dreadful in being killed in battle, amidst the fury and tumult of such a scene the mind cannot meditate with that tranquility which a Christian should desire on the coming awful change.'[3] These opinions were echoed later in the century when Pitt, whose history is in many ways a pacifist tract, complained that too much space was given to war in history books and added: 'Such history has no claim to be Christian.'[4] His whole aim was to prove that war is useless as well as foolish and that man has only advanced through the arts of peace.

The opinions of the 'pacific' school of writers, if such they may be called, are clearly seen in their descriptions of conquerors of various ages. Julius Caesar was one of those who received critical attention. In one book his career is described and then the author points out: 'Not selfish ambition, reckless of the rights of man . . . but the subordination of personal interest to the public good, justice to all, and mercy to the unfortunate are the qualities which give the most reasonable promise, as some of the claimants essential to true prosperity.'[5] William the Conqueror was also in many cases deplored as one whose evil seizure of power by force led to other cruelties.[6] Richard I was most unpopular with some authors. One described him as 'destitute of every moral quality'[7] and another declared that 'Richard cared too much about fighting to be a good king'.[8] Edward I also comes in for some sharp criticism. Bishop Davys remarked: 'I can never think of him without calling to mind his horrible cruelty. . . . But to such a king as Edward I, historians are generally ready to give a high character. And it is indeed true that his warlike spirit led him to perform such bright exploits as brought glory and greatness to his kingdom. But how little

---

1 Baldwin (1812), p. 16.
2 Markham (1874), p. 13.
3 Ibid. p. 425.
4 Pitt (1893), p. 8.
5 Milner (1852), p. 10.
6 Rodwell (1853), p. 39.
7 Legge (1864), p. 74.
8 *Cassells* (1884), p. 58.

does this contribute to the happiness of a people, compared with the peaceful, useful qualities which make a nation truly flourishing.'[1] At the end of the century, Miss Yonge also took a harsh view of Edward I's military exploits, and declared that when he advanced on Scotland 'he left his better self behind him'.[2] Likewise Edward III was adjudged guilty of starting an unjust war with France which caused, according to Mrs Ransome, 'much useless bloodshed'.[3]

Even with regard to these war heroes of the remote past, however, it is possible to trace a change of mood by the end of the century. Boadicea becomes something of a heroine to some writers: 'She stood in a war chariot, spear in hand with a bright collar round her neck. . . .'[4] Her efforts to cut the Romans to pieces are looked upon as something rather engaging: 'You would laugh if you could see one of the funny war chariots which they drove into the ranks of their enemies, for they had scythes tied to their wheels.'[5] Although Edward I is still often criticised for his warlike conduct, there are more favourable references to him, such as that in the *Holborn Readers*, which described him as having 'a true English heart, with a real love of his country'.[6] Complimentary opinions about the Black Prince are also more numerous towards the turn of the century, and Miss Yonge declared that the massacre of Limoges was 'the only really cruel act recorded of him'.[7]

It is in the selection of heroes that the authors of textbooks in the later nineteenth century really betray an admiration of the soldier, however. This is especially true of the readers intended for use in elementary schools, based as they were upon the requirements of the school code. For instance, in the *C.U.P. Reader* twenty-four out of the forty historical figures selected for study are primarily notable for their military prowess and several more are connected with major wars. The account of Florence Nightingale's life is concerned almost entirely with her work in the Crimea, and even Dick Whittington is singled out for his part in financing the Hundred Years War with an interest-free loan to Henry V, which he afterwards cancelled. In many of the readers the same material heroes,

---

[1] Davys (1822), p. 58.
[2] Yonge (1890), Book 3, p. 124.
[3] Ransome (1903), p. 117.
[4] *Cambridge* (1911), vol. 1, p. 99.
[5] Gill (1870), p. 4.
[6] Holborn (1885), Book 2, p. 64.
[7] Yonge (1890), vol. 3, p. 152.

notably Drake, Grenville, Marlborough, Wolfe, Clive, Nelson and Wellington, as well as the Victorian favourites Havelock and Gordon, are to be found. It is true that they are, to some extent, balanced by more peaceful heroes such as Stephenson and Wilberforce, but the latter are much in the minority.

Moreover, the heroes listed above were described in highly favourable terms towards the end of the nineteenth century. The author of the *Pitman Readers* forecast by way of introduction that: 'We shall read with pride of the good and valiant men, who either fought our country's battles against a foreign enemy, or strove against all attempts of tyrant rulers, to rob the people of their rights and liberties and even gave up their lives willingly in their noble efforts.'[1] Much praise was lavished on Cromwell, not mainly because of the merits of his domestic policy but because of the success which he achieved in making England powerful by his victories abroad: 'His name was feared, England respected and the cause of protestants defended throughout Europe.'[2] In contrast, England's feeble performance in battle during the reign of Charles II added to that monarch's evil reputation: 'As it is, there is no period in the history of England in which the patriot looks back with such burning shame and humiliation.'[3] Marlborough's victories were singled out for especial praise. The author of the *Holborn Readers* mentioned that the battle of Blenheim 'spread the fame of Marlborough and the English all over Europe and made his name a name to fear by every child in France.'[4] This sort of opinion about victory in battle did not pass without reproof from Pitt, who described the successes enjoyed by Marlborough in other words: 'He slew tens of thousands of his unoffending brother men, called "enemies".'[5] Nevertheless by the end of the nineteenth century Mrs Markham's view that 'if all people were true Christians, I believe there would be no conquerors'[6] was becoming unacceptable. Nelson, his adultery with Lady Hamilton forgotten, appeared as the prototype of the Christian warrior of whom Gordon and Havelock are seen as the finest examples: 'Now in the stories you have read you have seen that Nelson thought a great deal about duty; and that he was very brave and daring, and that he was also

---

[1] *Pitman* (1901), p. 6.
[2] *Cassells* (1883), p. 258.
[3] Gleig (1861), p 387.
[4] *Holborn* (1885), Book 2, p. 156.
[5] Pitt (1893), p. 72.
[6] Markham (1874), p. 125.

kind and tender-hearted.'[1] Havelock's death was described as if he were a martyr for his faith: 'His end was peace for he had lived a faithful follower of the Lord Jesus Christ.'[2] Miss Yonge is one of those who echo this attitude with regard to General Gordon and writes of the 'spirit that sustained him and made his death a victory of the soul and his name one that will live for ever more'.[3] Even Lord Raglan, a soldier not noted for his piety, was in one work described as 'a brave, good man' for his efforts in the Crimea.[4]

If opinions about killing and cruelty in war showed signs of change during the nineteenth century, however, the feeling that killing and cruelty on any other grounds were wrong persisted in general throughout the period. For instance, the racial and religious persecution of the Jews during the Middle Ages was frequently remarked on and condemned. It is true that at least one writer noted unsympathetically that Jews throughout the ages had retained their genius for pursuing gain and surviving in the face of danger,[5] and *Allison's Guide* mentioned the crucifixion as one reason why they were hated.[6] Most writers, however, used the terms 'atrocious massacre'[7] and 'infamous extortions' with reference to the persecution of the Jews, and Collier included a particularly colourful account of how 'the streets were slippery with Jewish blood' and the 'dying groans of God's ancient people could be heard'.[8]

Persecution on religious grounds is also condemned in those passages in the textbooks dealing with the persecutions of Mary I's reign. It is true that opinions about Mary are largely governed by protestant religious bias, nevertheless they do reveal a moral revulsion against cruelty in general and bigotted cruelty in particular. Some writers noted the violence of the Queen's temper,[9] and that 'the characteristics of Mary were bigotry and revenge'.[10] One concluded that: 'These atrocities turned the hearts of the people from a religion which could encourage such inhumanity',[11] though he does earlier state: 'Toleration was not then understood; neither was it

---

[1] *Cambridge* (1911), Book 1, p. 186.
[2] Curtis (1875), p. 155.
[3] Yonge (1890), vol. 6, p. 255.
[4] Laurie (1866), p. 262.
[5] Gleig (1853), pp. 96–7.
[6] *Allison* (1880), pp. 107–8.
[7] Curtis (1875), p. 36.
[8] Collier (1875), p. 78.
[9] Hort (1822), p. 157; Markham (1874), p. 271.
[10] Cooper (1843), p. 54.
[11] Morris (1883), p. 234.

anywhere practised.'[1] On the other hand, there was some attempt to lighten the picture of Mary's character by pointing out that her misdeeds made her unhappy. Airy's 'Whatever pain Mary inflicted on others she was probably the unhappiest woman in the kingdom' is a typical expression of this view.[2] The Catholic writer, Father Flanagan, was at pains to point out that Mary acted against the teachings of her own religion, if she was as cruel as people say, and he added: 'It was not until she had been provoked by repeated disturbances that she became at all severe.'[3] The view that Mary's conduct can be excused because of the danger she faced was echoed elsewhere.[4] Moreover, some writers were at pains to point out that Mary was cruel in religious matters, but otherwise exhibited the reverse virtues of kindliness and compassion. One remarked that she could be 'gentle and amiable' although he gives few signs of being pro-Catholic in attitude elsewhere.[5] In an Anglo-Catholic textbook Mary's faults were ascribed to her advisers, and she was described as 'one of the best, though not in the worldly sense, the greatest of English rulers'.[6]

In the case of Henry VIII's cruelty, which is depicted as being the result of mere caprice by many writers, opinions are even more condemnatory. Baldwin set the keynote early in the century when he noted that Henry 'was humorous and fantastical and in his fits of displeasure he spared neither friend nor foe'.[7] Similar judgments were expressed later: 'He quarrelled with everyone who opposed him and sent his best friends to the Tower when they disapproved of what he did.'[8] Moreover, Henry's cruelty was made worse for some writers by its association with his lust: 'His passions soothed by adulation, spurned all restraint and, as he was an utter stranger to the finer feelings of the soul, he gratified them at the expense of justice and humanity.'[9] So completely was Henry damned because of his self-indulgence and cruelty that condemnations of him range from the mild, 'not a person whom we can recommend others to love or to follow'[10] to the savage: 'A catalogue of the vices of Henry would comprehend many

---

[1] Morris (1883), p. 222.
[2] Airy (1898), p. 191.
[3] Flanagan (*c.* 1850), p. 54.
[4] Littlewoods (1869), p. 80.
[5] Legge (1864), p. 165.
[6] Baldwin (1812), p. 4.
[7] *English History for Children* (1845), p. 171.
[8] *Cassells Stories from English History* (1884), p. 106.
[9] Cooper (1843), p. 50.
[10] Farr (1856), p. 238.,

of the worst qualities incident to human nature.'[1] One or two writers did, it is true, see a lighter side of Henry. He was even depicted as a sort of evergreen public school boy: 'Men loved him for his bluff and frank ways and for his love of sport'[2] and one author commented that 'with all his caprice he remained firm to the last in his attachment to Cranmer'.[3] On the whole, however, the only people who really attempted to justify Henry's conduct in general were a small group of writers who considered, with Morris, that 'many of his acts are marked by cruelty and injustice, but his position was surrounded with the greatest difficulty, and harsh measures were sometimes necessary to save the country in the crisis through which it was then passing'.[4] To Mrs Ransome also it seemed that he might be viewed as a 'wise and patriotic King' as well as 'a heartless selfish tyrant'.[5] It is interesting that although the overwhelming majority of writers were aghast at the cruelty of both Mary and Henry VIII, a few did seek to justify their actions of the grounds of necessity. This argument was also used by those who would defend Elizabeth I from the many writers who accused her of the 'foul stain'[6] on her memory which was created by the execution of Mary, Queen of Scots. The author of the *Pitman Reader* considered the event 'one of the great blessings of English history'.[7]

Apart from cruelty the vice which was responsible for the most vehement opinions in history textbooks of the nineteenth century was sexual misconduct. This was in part a reaction against the luxury and licentiousness of the Regency period at the beginning of the century. One outward sign of this change can be seen in the attitude to the private conduct of men in public life. The Duke of Wellington, for instance, was not hounded out of society when he figured prominently in the memoirs of the famous courtesan, Harriet Wilson, which were first published in 1825, less than three years before he became Prime Minister. This contrasts with the fate of Parnell and Dilke who were deprived of office and influence in the 1880s because they were cited in divorce cases. By this time sexual immorality was associated with a range of other moral shortcomings, including dishonesty, cruelty and improvidence. The ideas of Dr Malthus, who

[1] *Blackwoods* (1883), vol. 2, p. 175.
[2] *History of England Mostly in Words of One Syllable* (1907), p. 48.
[3] Tegg (1862), p. 44.
[4] Morris (1883), p. 218.
[5] Ransome (1903), p. 189.
[6] Collier (1875), p. 180.
[7] *Pitman* (1901), p. 220.

raised fears that the country could not support its growing population, led to demands for greater sexual self-restraint, especially on the part of the working classes, in order to keep down the population. Moreover, as women were regarded as to some extent the property of their fathers or husbands, adultery and fornication were in some instances regarded as tantamount to stealing.

References to sexual behaviour in history books designed for use in schools were often guarded, especially in the more prudish years of Victoria's reign. There are, however, a surprising number of them. One of Alfred's virtues was, of course, that he was chaste—a fact implied by such phrases as 'virtuous'[1] or 'careful in his own life'.[2] Other rulers whose purity was sometimes remarked on include Charles I and his adversary, Cromwell. For instance, Carter compared the two men and wrote of Cromwell: 'Like Charles I his private life was simple, loving and pure',[3] while Grimaldi noted that the King, 'virtuous and exemplary in private life, was a good husband and father'.[4] This identification of chastity with a happy and secure background for children was most clearly stated in Mrs Markham's history where we find that Henry II's infidelities are blamed for the delinquency of his sons: 'My own opinion is that they acquired habits of disobedience to their father by seeing how little harmony subsisted between him and their mother.'[5] The same writer also identified chastity not with denial of sex but with a happy married life. Little Mary, on hearing that the clergy were not allowed to marry in the Middle Ages, cries out in horror: 'Oh, my dear Mama, what hard hearts the bishops of those times must have had.'[6]

When we consider sexual immorality rather than chastity as it appeared in the textbooks, however, we find that it was much more frequently commented upon than its obverse virtue and that opinions about it tended to be extremely condemnatory. It is perhaps surprising that so many traces of a more permissive attitude to sexual immorality can be found. Dodsley, of course, described Charles II's conduct in a ribald way which fully explains why Mrs Trimmer found his work so unsuitable to the young mind: 'Now it came to pass that Charles gave a loose to his appetites,

---

1 *Allison* (1880), p. 28.
2 *Cassells* (1883), p. 51.
3 Carter (1900), p. 209.
4 Grimaldi (1871), p. 146.
5 Markham (1874), p. 87.
6 Ibid. p. 68.

and indulged himself in all manner of delights, and he sent forth his pimps and nobles throughout all the land to search for the most beautiful women that could be found. . . . Now the king was pleased therewith and he was enamoured of them all; and he put forth his sceptre unto them, and the land was filled with royal bastards. . . . Moreover the nation, taking example from the court, ran headlong into all manner of licentiousness and immorality.'[1] It is notable that although Dodsley pays lip-service to orthodox morality, he refers to Charles' pleasures as 'delights'. Another example of a light-hearted attitude to the subject of sex is provided by Keightley who recounts that it was made treason for any wife of Henry VIII not to tell the king 'of any previous slip she might previously have made. It was jocularly said that the king must not look now for any but a widow'.[2] Several, whose works were published in the earlier years of the nineteenth century, took a mild and even approving attitude towards Henry II's illicit affair with Rosamund Clifford. Baldwin remarked that 'to console himself for this misfortune (the savage temper of his wife) he attached himself to a very beautiful lady called fair Rosamund by whom he had several children'.[3] Much the same line was taken by the authors of *Allison's Guide*,[4] and the *Catechism of English History*,[5] while Cooper re-marked that Henry was 'brave, learned, prudent, polite, generous and of a mild disposition, but these virtues did not exempt him from suffering the greatest vexations even in his own family. Attachment to the fair sex was his predominant passion.'[6] As we shall see, such a view is in sharp contrast to that of many later writers who assume that because a man is unchaste he has all the other vices too. Here the reverse is the case and Henry is endowed with all manner of virtues which it is doubtful he really displayed. It is notable that all these examples of tolerance of sexual misconduct date from the first half of the nineteenth century and it is probable that the stricter attitude to sexual immorality in Victoria's reign accounts for their subsequent disappearance.

Even when dealing with a pre-Christian era some writers demonstrated their attachment to the Christian sexual ethic. Gleig, for instance, com-mented in horror on the nudity of the ancient Britons, and added: 'Men

---

[1] Dodsley (1799), pp. 113–14.
[2] Keightley (1841), p. 136.
[3] Baldwin (1812), p. 356.
[4] *Allison* (1880 ed.), p. 92.
[5] *Catechism of English History* (1810), p. 37.
[6] Cooper (1843), p. 11.

and women lived together in a state of promiscuous intercourse, so that children knew not their parents nor the parents their children. Whenever such a state of society prevails, it were vain to search for institutions to which the terms employed in describing the usages of civilized life can properly be applied.'[1] From the outset, therefore, Gleig identifies civilisation with monogamy. Bishop Davys, too, emerges as an opponent of those of his time who would tolerate Henry II's philandering, and he demonstrates clearly how sexual immorality may be linked to other sins: 'Henry had caused Becket to be put to death and had neglected his wife that he might live with Rosamund. Here is murder and adultery.'[2] The tendency to suggest that the licentious man is guilty of all other crimes can also be seen in Collier's description of Edward IV. 'His lustful passions brought shame to many an honest household. Gorgeous dresses, rich meats, costly wines were among his highest enjoyments. He waded to the throne in blood and maintained it by a spy system.'[3] George IV, though a comparatively recent ruler, was not spared the blame for his sexual misconduct which brought on him almost complete condemnation. 'He was an unprincipled and dissolute man who set the worst example to all classes by his wild behaviour.'[4] Frequently the writers seem to imply that licentious behaviour is among the worst of all crimes, and it is perhaps significant that in spite of their dislike of rebellion many writers stressed the 'insult' offered to Wat Tyler's daughter by the lustful tax-collector[5] and seem to approve the outraged father's conduct in striking him dead on the spot.

As might be expected, Charles II comes in for some very savage criticism. The tone was set early in the nineteenth century with Cooper's damning description of him. 'He was a scoffer at religion, and a libertine in morals, careless, indolent, profuse, abandoned to effeminate pleasure, incapable of any noble enterprise, a stranger to manly friendship and gratitude, deaf to the voice of honour, blind to the allurements of glory and, in a word, destitute of every active virtue.'[6] Cooper's accusations were frequently echoed by other writers. In his character, it seems, were united all the qualities that nineteenth-century writers found most hateful. They expressed their horror at his love of female company—'He kept a great

---

[1] Gleig (1853), p. 4.
[2] Davys (1822), p. 26.
[3] Collier (1875), p. 136.
[4] *Cassells* (1883), p. 356.
[5] Morris (1882), p. 118.
[6] Cooper (1830), p. 83.

many mistresses, actresses, opera dancers and others'[1]—in terms which suggest that part of his disgrace was the lowly social station of his companions. Furthermore, he was seen as responsible for the fact that in his reign 'earnest religion and virtue were scoffed at'.[2] Even his death-bed repentance was not admired since it made him a papist, so bringing his ignominious career to a final sordid close: 'After a life of disgraceful vice and tyrannic oppression, Charles II died in communion with the Church of Rome.'[3] The fact that Charles was not ashamed of his conduct and did not try to conceal it gave special offence to many writers: 'It caused him no shame to do wrong', wrote the author of the *History of England Mostly in Words of One Syllable*,[4] and Farr described how the King 'abandoned himself to sensual enjoyments',[5] being one of a group of writers who seem to believe that Charles's evident enjoyment of his wicked conduct was one of his worst features. Furthermore, his lechery was made worse by its association with extravagance, and several authors refer to Charles's 'excessive gaiety, immorality and extravagance',[6] or point out that his 'debauched way of living was very expensive'.[7] Part of Charles's evil reputation also rested on the fact that his immoral conduct was associated with lack of success in and enthusiasm for foreign wars.[8] This is no doubt the 'noble enterprise' and 'allurement of glory' which Cooper criticised Charles for resisting.[9]

It is this combination of evil qualities which made the reign of Charles II seems such a dreadful one to many writers. In *Allison's Guide* the question is put: 'What was the character of his reign?' to be followed by the stern reply: 'It was the most immoral and disgraceful in English history', and the *Collins History* agreed: 'It was the most dissolute period of our history.'[10] Bishop Davys went further and pointed out that all this sin did not pass without divine retribution. 'We cannot help thinking that, by the fire and pestilence, the Almighty punished a profligate nation for its sins; but that is his mercy.'[11]

---

[1] Baldwin (1812), p. 117.
[2] Bullock (1861), p. 160.
[3] Hort (1822), pp. 283-4.
[4] 1907, p. 65.
[5] Farr (1856), p. 322.
[6] Corner (1885), p. 320.
[7] Baldwin (1812), p. 118.
[8] See above p. 74.
[9] Cooper (1830), p. 83.
[10] *Collins* (1890), p. 151.
[11] Davys (1822), p. 201.

A small group of writers, however, could find a few pleasant things to say of Charles. One left the questionable moral aspects of Charles's life aside, remarking that 'of greater ability than his father, Charles II had added to his natural sagacity and tact a wide experience of men and things'.[1] Another ventured a slight compliment: 'He had been a bad man and a bad king; yet his gay and affable manners had made him popular.'[2] The Roman Catholic writer, Livesey, remarked that Charles never lost his religious faith, however badly he might have acted. Female authors were, in general, lenient towards Charles. It is extremely surprising, indeed, to find the redoubtable Mrs Trimmer venturing a faint word of praise—'Not naturally destitute of good and noble feelings'—amid the criticism,[3] and Miss Yonge sympathetically noted that Charles was 'easily led' and 'had kindly words for all so that most people liked him'.[4] Not only those ladies who perhaps inclined to Tory devotion to the monarchy, but also others who are in general on the 'Whig' side express sympathy for him. Mrs Ransome believed that 'most people thought him a gay, careless, pleasure-loving man and had no idea of real cleverness and strength of will hidden behind his charming manner and easy-going ways',[5] while Miss Rolleston declared him 'clever' though 'unprincipled'[6] and the Misses Conan and Kendall wrote that 'He was witty and graceful, fond of women and dogs', though they also criticised him for his cynical disregard of the feelings of others.[7]

Kings of homosexual rather than heterosexual tastes are also severely dealt with, though their offences are of course almost unmentionable and have to be sketched in obliquely. One writer declared that William Rufus 'never married and was a very bad and wicked man',[8] and elsewhere it is noted that because of his sins, no one was sorry for Rufus's death.[9] Edward II came in for criticism because his friends were not drawn from a suitably high social class and Fletcher painted a vivid picture of how he 'hung on the neck of a low-class Gascon favourite who made fun of the sober English barons until they caught and killed him'.[10] There was comment on the

---

[1] Hassall (1901), p. 382.
[2] Keightley (1841), p. 81.
[3] Trimmer (1849), p. 251.
[4] Yonge (1890), vol. 5, p. 95.
[5] Ransome (1903), p. 281.
[6] Rolleston (1902), p. 193.
[7] Conan and Kendall (1902), p. 296.
[8] Tegg (1862), p. 12.
[9] *Cambridge* (1911), p. 49.
[10] Fletcher and Kipling (1911), p. 90.

frivolous foreigner's disgraceful ways: 'When you hear a boy call nick-names, you may be pretty sure that he is of a mean and sneaking disposi-tion. Much more is this the case, when a full-grown man (unworthy of the name) practises so silly a habit.'[1] Several writers gave hair-raising descrip-tions of the savage end which Edward's sins called forth, including 'the screams with which the agonising king filled the castle while his bowels were consuming'.[2] In general, a tactful veil was drawn over the nature of the conduct of those kings who may have indulged in homosexual practices, but Morris is one writer who delicately underlines them by comparing the conduct of William Rufus and Richard I and then of Edward II and Richard II.[3]

It is interesting that the attitudes displayed in textbooks towards the sexual conduct of important female historical figures do seem somewhat more lenient than towards their male counterparts. A man's success in the world was partly measured by the degree of idleness in which he could keep his womenfolk. As a result the womanly virtues did not ideally include powers of decision or determination or too much display of intelligence. Mr Gladstone, for instance, refused to lend his support to the cause of obtaining voting rights for women on the grounds that they would 'trespass upon their delicacy, their purity, their refinement, the elevation of their whole nature'.[4] Likewise Charlotte M. Yonge replied to a letter from Emily Davies, who had hoped to enlist her support for attempts to found a women's college, by stating that girls were best educated at home under the influence of their parents. 'All the most superior women I have known have been thus formed by *home* influence, and I think that girls in large numbers always hurt one another in manner and tone if in nothing else.'[5] It was perhaps partly owing to her charming femininity as well as to the influence of the romantic movement in literature that Mary, Queen of Scots, generally escaped censure.

In spite of the disadvantages of being a Roman Catholic and the object of suspicions of murder, treason and adultery, she was on the whole well regarded and her death was much lamented. It is true she was referred to as 'a wanton, unprincipled woman'[6] and 'rash and impudent'.[7] Neverthe-

---

[1] Birkby (1869), p. 48.
[2] Hume (1875), p. 71.
[3] Morris (1883), pp. 93–136.
[4] Quoted in *Ideas-Beliefs of the Victorians* (1949), p. 267.
[5] Quoted in *The Victorians*, edited by J. Evans (1966), p. 119.
[6] *Allison* (1880), p. 308.
[7] Keightley (1841), p. 154.

less few writers condemned her wholly. Ince and Gilbert might declare that 'she had the credit of but few qualities either estimable or amiable', but they added: 'And yet she was devotedly sincere in her attachment to the Roman Catholic faith, was susceptible of true friendship and in many instances, gave undoubted proofs of her resolution and vigour'.[1] Even Mrs Markham, though obviously shocked at Mary's stormy marital career, remarked: 'When we bear in mind the conditions of Mary's early education we may find some excuses for her great misconduct. She had acquired in France a taste for elegance, but had at the same time learned a disregard for decorum, if not a familiarity with vice.'[2] So Mary was portrayed as the victim of a foreign upbringing. The *Granville Readers*, admittedly a Catholic publication, described the feelings of those present at her death: 'Most likely they were all glad that the beautiful and unhappy Mary, after her long life of sorrow, was gone where no cruelty could reach her any more.'[3] At the opposite end of the religious spectrum of opinion, Milner (of the Religious Tract Society) wrote of the Babington Plot 'of which advantage was taken to terminate the life and sorrows of the Queen of Scots'.[4] He went on to stress the unfairness of her trial and the dignity of her bearing at her execution.

In contrast Elizabeth I, who was certainly no more unchaste and self-indulgent in her conduct than Mary, received some sharp criticism. It is true that she is occasionally much admired. Keightley, for instance, describes her as 'the glory of her sex and the brightest ornament of English history'.[5] Also those who criticise her often admitted: 'She certainly understood the art of governing in an eminent degree.'[6] On the other hand, she is accused by many writers of undue harshness towards Mary, Queen of Scots. Otherwise the main charges against her are extravagance and sexual licence. Gleig, for instance, wrote of her 'infirmities of temper and disposition' and added: 'In private life her most ardent admirer cannot acquit her of conduct which, to say the least of it, was extremely unbecoming.'[7] It may be that Elizabeth's outstanding intellect and rejection of the married state struck the Victorians as somewhat indecorous. Tait gives

---

1 Ince and Gilbert (1859), p. 84.
2 Markham (1874), p. 286.
3 Granville (1885), p. 63.
4 Milner (1854), p. 467.
5 Keightley (1841), p. 152.
6 Cooper (1843), p. 60.
7 Gleig (1853), p. 293.

some support to this view by the way in which he stressed Elizabeth's intellect and linked it with the opinion that she was emotionally cold: 'Beneath her love of pleasure and flattery, her nature was purely intellectual, hard as steel, untinctured by the affections.'[1] Several writers stressed her vanity and extravagant love of finery: 'She delighted in finery and wore splendid dresses and costly jewels. It is said that when she died, nearly three thousand dresses were found in her wardrobe. But she had the weaknesses of a vain woman.'[2] Perhaps the prevailing attitude to Elizabeth is best summed up by Miss Rolleston: 'As a woman Elizabeth was not lovable. She was vain heartless and even at times indecorous in the freedom of her manners.'[3]

The stress on extravagance which we find in the descriptions of the careers of Elizabeth, Charles II and others is part of what might be termed the 'middle-class morality' of the textbook writers. Apart from sexual licence and waste, they deplored a whole range of vices which they held to be associated with irresponsible attitudes to society and advancement within it. These included idleness, lying, over-indulgence in food and drink, smoking, swearing and gambling. For example, Charles I is much criticised for his failure to keep his word during the negotiations with Parliament, his 'perfidy'.[4] Other instances of dishonesty and its evil consequences were drawn, for example, from the life of Henry III. Miss Yonge described how 'the king did not keep his word, so that at last no one had any trust in what he said and he did almost as much harm as if he had been a bad, cruel man, like his father King John'.[5] Laziness was also occasionally mentioned as the cause of retribution. Lord North, blamed for the loss of the American colonies, was depicted as 'lazy and indolent and like other men of that time, was too fond of drinking wine and playing cards'.[6] In contrast, hard-working characters, such as Alfred, were much admired for their 'industry'.[7] To judge from his selection of notable historical figures, Pringle, the author of *Local Examination History*, was particularly anxious to stress the example of men who had risen from comparatively humble circumstances by their own hard work. For

---

[1] Tait (1878), p. 88.
[2] Holborn (1882), vol. 2, pp. 112–13.
[3] Rolleston (1902), p. 108.
[4] Curtis (1885), p 113.
[5] Yonge (1890), vol. 3, pp. 35–6.
[6] *Cassells' Simple Outline* (1884), p. 157.
[7] Allison (1880), p. 28.

[85]

instance, he particularly mentions Whewell, the son of a carpenter who became Master of King's College, Cambridge.[1]

Indeed the manners and amusement of society in the past were much criticised for their failure to measure up to the sober standards of Victorian times. The author of *Allison's Guide* inquired with reference to George II's reign: 'What sensual habits prevailed?' and provided the reply: 'Smoking and drunkenness. Gentlemen rarely met at dinner without drinking to intoxication.'[2] This was remarked on elsewhere: 'During the last fifty years an entire change has fortunately taken place in the habits of good society and a gentleman of the old school would not now be tolerated in decent society.'[3] Even William Pitt the Younger did not go uncriticised for his weakness for drink: 'His life was unstained by vice, unless we consider his indulgence in port-wine to be one.'[4] Greediness for food was also commented on unfavourably. John is, of course, a cautionary example of this vice: 'Fortunately at this juncture he died suddenly of a fever, brought on by exposure and greediness.'[5] So is Henry I: 'I must tell you the cause of his death; for I think it is a good lesson to all of us. He had been told by his physicians that he ought not to eat too much, but one day a favourite dish was brought to his table ... and he ate such a quantity that it made him ill and so he died. ...'[6]

Gambling and other sports also called forth much criticism in textbooks of the nineteenth century. It is true that there were a few moderate views such as that of Beale who blamed the effects of Cromwell's 'unscriptural prohibition of innocent amusements' for the excesses of Charles II's reign which followed.[7] On the other hand, Bishop Davys inveighed against the horrors of gambling: 'Whenever there is anything like gambling, it generally leads to ruin; or if some few have got rich by it, I have observed that their riches seldom do them any good. And the money-making schemes of George I's time, indeed, in many instances, introduced riches into the country, but these riches led to extravagance and covetousness, and a great deal of covetousness and wickedness.'[8] Similarly, Hume's *Continuator*

---

[1] Pringle (1907), p. 163.
[2] *Allison* (1880), p. 386.
[3] Morris (1883), p. 519.
[4] Rolleston (1902), p. 202.
[5] Conan and Kendall (1902), p. 89.
[6] Callcott (1962), p 57.
[7] Beale (1858), p. 168.
[8] Davys (1822), p. 236.

[86]

stressed the decline in gambling and prize-fighting as he explained the general improvement in the nation's morals.[1]

The connection between gambling and drinking and social disgrace is perhaps well illustrated by this verdict on George IV: 'But if gambling, drinking, prize-fighting, lying, cheating at cards and a disreputable private life make even a king a blackguard, then George certainly was one.' Swearing is also sometimes mentioned as a social offence. Reference was made to the 'obscene oath's which used to disgrace society in the past[2] and it was noted that this vice disappeared from the hospital at Scutari under the benign rule of Miss Nightingale and her nurses.[3]

We must, however, beware of the assumption that generally expressed views on morality were those adopted by society as a whole. The most famous women of the Victorian era tend to those who, like Florence Nightingale or George Eliot, defied their families or society. The researches of Mayhew and Stead, the author of *Maiden Tribute*, showed the prevalence of prostitution despite the horror expressed at sexual immorality. Even the minor vice of smoking was on the increase as a *Times* leader for 1861 remarked.[4] By the end of the nineteenth century one writer was bewailing the fact that there was a decline rather than a growth of 'old-fashioned honesty', and an increase 'of impertinence and the habit of gambling'. He complained that people who would not steal or pick a pocket would cheat the bus and railway companies by not paying their fares or keep lost property they had found, or cheat their employer in some minor way. He went on: 'Mothers are no longer so stern about truth-speaking in their children. . . . When it is held to be sufficient excuse for a theft that the thief was in need of bread, it becomes an easy transition to justify any action by which a poor man is benefitted at the expense of a rich one'.[5] However, if Victorian England was not so 'moral' as it wished to be, its attitude to the poor was not so condemnatory and unfeeling as it sometimes pretended. It is true that some suggested that the money spent on poor relief was wasted on drink and debauchery,[6] but large sums of money were devoted to the welfare of the poor by private charities. The religious impulse to works of mercy was strong in Christians of all denominations

---

1 Hume (1875), p. 741.
2 Morris (1883), p. 519.
3 Holborn (1882), vol. 1, p. 67.
4 Quoted in *The Victorians*, edited by J. Evans (1966), p. 119.
5 Ibid. pp. 44-45.
6 Ibid. p. 45.

during the nineteenth century and some of these were not slow to point out that the miseries of the poor were not entirely or merely due to their own sins. In a sermon preached during the Irish Famine of 1846, Dr Pusey, one of the founders of the Oxford Movement, asserted: 'In its turn, luxury is the parent of covetousness; and covetousness of unjust gain, and of the grinding of the poor. We *will* not limit our self-indulgence; and so in order to obtain it cheaply, we pare down the wages of our artisans.'[1]

It is perhaps illuminating that the moral tone of society is so firmly identified in most textbooks with virtues such as sobriety, industry and thrift rather than with care for the weak and under-privileged. As we have seen, opinions about the poor, especially when the Poor Law is discussed, tended to be extremely harsh and unsympathetic. The few social reformers who were chosen to appear as leading figures in English history include Hanway, Howard and Elizabeth Fry, but by far the most common is Wilberforce. Sympathetic reference is often made to the plight of African slaves; there is considerably less comment on efforts to alleviate the plight of factory children in England, a fact actually noted in a reader published during the First World War.[2] Of the books examined, none took Lord Shaftesbury as a 'hero' figure, and only one had a long section on the life of factory children. The author of this reader is also unique in asserting that the reformer, Howard, who risked his health in a tour of prisons, was as brave as any soldier.[3]

A small group of writers did, however, stress the importance of social reform, connecting it especially with religious belief. Cobbett, as we have remarked, identified social injustice with the coming of the Reformation, and traced back to it 'that misery, that beggary, that nakedness, that hunger, that everlasting wrong-doing and spite which now stare us in the face'.[4] No other early writer seems to mount such a thorough attack on the character of society because of its indifference to the state of the poor and downtrodden. However, Corkran claimed that the condition of England would always be hopeful so long as 'social morality and philanthropy show themselves in the creation of institutions adapted to meet all human wants'.[5] Milner even went so far as to suggest that all was not well with the condition of 'the operative classes' in his own time, though he saw a lighter

[1] Quoted in *The Victorians*, edited by J. Evans (1966), p. 224.
[2] *Oxford History Readers* (1916), vol VIII, p. 35.
[3] *Chambers* (1901–5), vol III, p. 119.
[4] Cobbett (1823), introduction, para. 1.
[5] Corkran (1859), pp. 302–4.

[88]

side to the picture too: 'If error stalks abroad, while sin is rife, and wretchedness abounds, there is a gratifying amount of Christian virtue, piety and benevolence round the neighbourhood of the evil to subdue it.'[1] By the early years of this century expressions of concern with social justice had come to appear more frequently, especially in elementary school readers. One writer boasted that: 'There is far more sympathy with the poor and helpless than there used to be.'[2]

It certainly seems that in the years immediately preceding the First World War history textbooks contained a variety of conflicting opinions indicative of changing moral standards in society as a whole. Disapproval of war was on the wane, indeed the war-hero was now a figure of admiration; and there was a growing tendency for cruelty and violence to be justified in terms of expediency. Yet at the same time there was a growing concern for the poorer sections of society. Indeed, it is a feature of the textbooks that they reflect a world of changing rather than merely dogmatic moral judgments. While it is true that many of these such as the strictures against laziness, dishonesty, gluttony, drunkenness and unchastity accorded well with the Victorian concern to 'civilize' the working classes into law-abiding workers and citizens, there is very little difference in the character or in the force of moral opinions expressed in books for middle- and working-class children, as one might possibly expect if writers had had a propagandist aim. Moreover, certain of the attitudes which commonly appeared, for instance the distaste for war or bloodshed, did not necessarily coincide with what was convenient for Victorian governments or indeed those of modern times. In our own age it is difficult to understand the dogmatic certainty and moral earnestness of some of these opinions. To do so it is necessary to consider the character of Victorian religious belief and its effects on the aims of education.

---

[1] Milner (1854), p. 802.
[2] *Cambridge* (1911), p. 282.

CHAPTER IV

Religious Opinions

'However, in England there were a great many good
men on both sides.'[1]

To the Victorians religion offered both a cement for society and a scapegoat for its shortcomings in the past. It was commonly assumed that there was a strong connection between unorthodoxy or disbelief and moral and political disruption. Brougham, for instance, referred in 1827 to the Radicals as: 'A set of drivellers. . . . They are in their religion intolerable aetheists, in their politics bloody-minded republicans, and in morals somewhat gross, and most selfish latitudinarians.'[2] It is partly for this reason that such concern was shown over religious bias in history textbooks and that pains were taken to conceal the advance of agnosticism, though undoubtedly the age was one of sincere and zealous religious conviction in many quarters. The role of scapegoat was, however, filled not by the forces of unbelief but by the Church of Rome. It was this which was primarily identified with the forces of social and political reaction, with moral decadence and with foreign treachery.[3] Many authors were content to dwell in colourful phrases on the iniquities of this old enemy. In this they may have been encouraged by the influence of the evangelical movement with its emphasis on zeal, emotion in religion and its distaste for Roman Catholicism.

At the beginning of the nineteenth century there still remained within the established Church and the protestant dissenting sects many traces of the cool and rational approach to the discussion of religion which had largely characterised the previous century. Still influential were the ideas of such divines as Joseph Butler and George Berkeley who had defended their beliefs in an unemotional and rational manner, remaining relatively tolerant of those who did not share them. Enthusiasm in religion as in

---

[1] Callcott (1875), p. 148.
[2] Quoted in *The Age of Reform*, by E. L. Woodward (1938), p. 66.
[3] See 'Popular Protestantism in Victorian Britain', by G. F. A. Best, in *Ideas and Institutes of Victorian Britain*, pp. 115–42.

other matters was distrusted. A similar mode of thought is to be traced in the ideas of dissenters such as the unitarian, Priestley. For him education was a means of ensuring the future well-being of the pupil in this life rather than in the world to come. 'The chief and proper object of education is not to form a *shining* and *popular* character; but a *useful* one, this being also the only foundation of true happiness.'[1] Likewise Chapman stressed the importance of education as 'a powerful influence on human happiness'.[2]

Already in the eighteenth century there were signs of an emotional reaction against the rational approach to religion. Law's *Serious Call to a Devout and Holy Life* and the growth and success of the Methodist movement under the leadership of John Wesley is evidence of this. The Evangelical movement within the Church of England, led by Wilberforce, Hannah More and others who composed what became known as the Clapham sect, re-emphasised the emotional aspects of Christian belief in the early years of the ninteenth century. Claiming that they based their tenets on the literal interpretation of the Bible, they stressed the need for purity of conduct as a sign of personal commitment to God. The existence of an after-life where the saved received their due reward and the damned their punishment, was also held to be a belief of extreme importance. For the Evangelicals education was not merely designed as a preparation for life, but also as a preparation for eternity. They emphasised that the teaching of Christianity was central to the training of the young. 'The Christian religion, then, the first and the last, the greatest and best of all human concerns, cannot without equal guilt and folly be neglected in education. It should indeed pervade its beginning, its progress and its end.'[3] One corollary of this idea was that the young must be protected from pagan or atheist ideas. As we have seen, Hannah More attacked Hume's history on the ground that any work written by one of his scepticism must be untrustworthy,[4] and she elsewhere refers to pagan history as of little value compared to Christian, though she does not declare it to be entirely without use.[5] Although most of the leaders of the Clapham sect were dead by 1840, the influence of the Evangelical movement was seen to the end of the nineteenth century in the stress on reading the Bible, attendance at church and prayers, and a high standard of moral conduct which was widely

---

[1] *Miscellaneous Observations on Education*, by J. Priestley (1812 ed.), p. xi.
[2] *A Treatise on Education*, by G. Chapman (1790), p. v.
[3] *Essay on Education*, by W. Barrow (1802), pp. 195–6.
[4] More's *Hints* (1805), p. 157.
[5] Ibid. p. 63.

accepted in the middle and upper classes of Victorian society at least. There was a feeling in the middle years of the century that the nation was by and large a Christian one and as such played a special role in God's purpose. As a reviewer in the *Educational Times* wrote: 'England has a more perfect system of religion than pagan times allowed and there can be no doubt of the focus, the centre of what may be termed a new phase of civilisation.'[1]

At the opposite extreme there stood the group of those who had come to reject religious belief altogether or which held grave doubts of its validity. During the nineteenth century this gained in influence and social respectability. At first atheism was identified with revolutionary radicals, such as Tom Paine, and therefore widely deplored. With the growth of scientific discovery, especially the evolutionary theories of Darwin which were seen to conflict with a literal interpretation of the Bible, scepticism among the educated classes began to revive. As one Victorian put it: '. . . though the development of the theory be not atheistic, it is at least practically tantamount to atheism. For, if man be a dying creature, restricted in his existence to the present scheme of things, what does it really matter to him, for any moral purpose, whether there be a God or no?'[2] Later in the century the writings of Matthew Arnold and T. H. Huxley, among others, served to make agnosticism intellectually and socially respectable. At the same time Bradlaugh fought for and, by 1886 won the right of atheists to affirm allegiance instead of taking the Parliamentary oath. As we have seen, the textbook author, W. S. Ross, was an associate of Bradlaugh's before they quarrelled.[3] He aided the work of publicising rationalist or atheist views and was particularly forthright in his expressions of dislike and contempt for organised religion. In a speech at the inauguration of the Whitminster Secular School in 1886, Ross referred to the priest as a 'carrion bird of ill-omen' and spoke of the new rationalist creed which would 'superseding the dark and ghastly cross upon Mount Calvary work out the first true redemption of the human race'.[4] In fact by the end of the nineteenth century there was considerable tolerance of anti-religious points of view. This, combined with the laxer moral attitudes to be found in the upper ranks of society following the example of the Prince of Wales, all served to weaken the hold

---

[1] 1855, p. 205.
[2] Quoted in *The Victorians*, edited by J. Evans (1966), p. 223.
[3] See earlier, p. 23-4.
[4] Whitminster Secular School Inauguration (reprinted from the *Secular Review*), p. 6.

of orthodox religion on the influential sections of the population—a fact remarked upon by A. V. Dicey in 1905.[1]

By the last quarter of the nineteenth century indeed there were many who deplored the religious bias to be found in history textbooks. An advertisement commended Schmitz's textbook because it seemed to be without 'any political, theological or ecclesiastical bias, which affect so many of our school histories and render them unsuitable to be put into the hands of the young'. To the modern reader the work does seem very moderate in tone, though dull.[2] In a later edition of the same periodical T. C. Curtis's *Elements in the History of England* was reviewed,[3] and praised, not for lack of any political bias, but because it gave a fair measure of attention to 'such parts of our country's origin and growth which are not associated with Scripture history'. The same wish to avoid over-stressing the religious element in history and the curriculum in general can be traced in *Lectures on Teaching*, by J. G. Fitch,[4] then an inspector of schools. He commented favourably on teachers who 'dread above all things exacting from a young child vows or professions of religion which cannot correspond to his actual convictions and experience'. This group, he believed, would wish to teach religion and morality from the whole tone of the school and its work rather than through lessons in divinity or scripture.

In contrast, for some textbook writers throughout the century, history was seen as the working of God through events, and they held that it should be taught as such. In answer to a question about the use of history, Mrs Markham replied: 'The older you grow and the more you read of it, the better you will be able to understand its use. I shall only say now that the greatest and best use of it is to show us by observing events as they follow, the greatness and wisdom of God and how wonderfully he ordereth the affairs of men.'[5] Other writers were even more explicit about the action of 'Divine Providence' in history. One declared: 'Hence its record is not rightly read, if curiosity alone be gratified, or interest excited by it. As the exponent of Providence, speaking to nations and individuals of those immutable laws of God's moral judgment which eventually connect pains and penalties with delinquency and guilt, while awarding true prosperity to public and private goodliness, the legitimate effect of

---

[1] *Law and Opinion in England* (1905), p. 465.
[2] 7 June 1873, p. 408.
[3] 4 March 1876, p. 237.
[4] *Lectures on Teaching*, by J. G. Fitch (1885), p. 427.
[5] Markham (1874), p. 14.

veritable history is alone produced when the mind is fortified by its events to obey the inspired maxim "cease to do evil; learn to do well".[1] Here the link between religious belief and the moral code in evangelical eyes is made absolutely clear.

Another aspect of this was the widespread feeling that God had been particularly merciful towards the English people. This was seen in the coming of the Reformation which showed the 'revealed will of God', so that the nation had since prospered in proportion to its obedience to it.[2] Bishop Davys was particularly fulsome in his praise for the goodness of God to the English. 'How thankful we ought to be that the knowledge of the Gospel, which is still kept from many nations, has been given to *us*! and how anxious we ought to be to show ourselves worthy of so great a gift by the effect that it produces on our lives and practices! How thankful ought we to be that we have churches to go to and how regular ought we to be in seeking to bring others to the knowledge and love of the same faith whether they be ignorant or the profane in our own land, or the unconverted and unenlightened among the heathen.'[3] Although this represents a rather extreme expression of devotion to the Christian faith and its propagation the same opinion is sometimes to be traced in books in use in public schools and colleges or the home during the nineteenth century, as well as in elementary school readers. One writer remarked that the first of blessings is to be born a Christian; the second is to be born English.[4]

Only rarely was any attack made on accepted Christian opinions. One writer, it is true, did stress that the historian must not seek to find retributive justice always obviously at work in history, but he still considered that the 'laws of action and reaction' which he put in its place were 'divinely established'.[5] In this connection, it is particularly interesting to search for traces of anti-Christian thought in the work of the atheist, Ross. He did criticise the bishops for their opposition to the 1832 Reform Bill: 'It was too practical to recommend itself to the Lords Spiritual and they opposed it in a Christian phalanx.'[6] However, condemnation of the bishops, though not found in other writers, need not necessarily be an indication of anti-Christian bias. Possibly he took refuge in irony, since the exclamation

---

[1] Milner (1856), p. 2.
[2] Curtis (1875), p. 172.
[3] Davys (1822), p. 7.
[4] Laurie (1866), p. 266.
[5] Beale (1858), p. v.
[6] Ross (1872), p. 60.

'Oh, was there indeed no God in heaven!'[1] on the execution of Marie Antoinette may be more than the dramatic touch which it appears on the surface. It is, indeed, very difficult to tell whether Ross is really serious in some of his expressions of opinion on religious and other matters. What are we to make of this passage from the pen of such a well-known free-thinker, except, perhaps, that it may savour of protesting too much? 'One thing may be said of all the churches, that they are animated by the noblest spirit of philanthropy and enlightened benevolence and that their increasing efforts to rescue the lower classes from immorality, to educate and train the young, to spread the softening influence of Christianity to other lands and to counteract the secularizing influences of our daily life by implanting devoted and ennobling thoughts and leading our minds to the contemplation of Divine Truth are usually of the highest esteem and admiration.'[2] Ross's work is, in fact, an example of the way in which the commercial market imposes its own censorship on ideas which, like his atheism, were much at variance with the prevailing opinions of the times.

In history textbooks references to those who opposed Christianity were confined to a passing mention of Voltaire and the rationalism which led to the Revolution in France[3] or to the cynicism of Charles II's reign as described by Dodsley: 'and whereas before they used to seek the Lord and implore His direction even in the most trifling affairs, it was now deemed almost superstitious to believe in Him.'[4] In contrast the defenders of the Christian faith in England were much commended. George III, for example, was praised for his intentions regarding Bible-reading among his subjects: 'To his lasting honour, he avowed the wish that everyone of his subjects might possess a copy of the Holy Scriptures with the ability to read the word of eternal life.'[5] Wesley and his followers were especially admired for their work in saving England from unbelief. Pringle, not otherwise notably a writer of strong religious views, remarked: 'To them we owe the great renewal of religion that had its birth in this reign.'[6] Elsewhere the Wesleyans were credited with making the English think more about religion and altering their conduct for the better.[7]

No topic is more revealing as to the changing value put upon Christianity

---

[1] Ibid. p. 23.
[2] Ibid. p. 131.
[3] Gleig (1853), p. 522.
[4] Dossley (1796), p. 115.
[5] Milner (1856), p. 768.
[6] Pringle (1907), p 114.
[7] *Warwick*, vol. 5, p. 55 (1891).

as opposed to paganism than the coming of Christianity to England. One or two writers early in the century betray traces of a somewhat latitudinarian attitude to the pagans, who were depicted in such a way as to bring out their similarities to Christians: 'As the time when the Druids flourished in Britain was before Christ, they could not be Christians, they were very devout, said many prayers, sang many hymns, and made many sacrifices. I am sorry to say that they sometimes sacrificed (that is killed) men at their altars and thought to please God by it.'[1] Miss Rodwell, later in the century also gave the ancient Britons sympathetic treatment, emphasising that they could not help their ignorance and even playing down the cruelty of their religious practices. 'You who say your prayers night and morning will think it strange that the Britons did not know that there is a God who is great and good . . . the poor Britons, who knew no better . . . used to pray to the trees because they thought some of the Gods were there.'[2]

It never occurred to other writers to wonder why the Britons were left in ignorance of the true religion. Instead they were frequently criticised for their failure to measure up to Christian standards of morality. As we have seen, Gleig looked with horror on the sexual promiscuity and nudity of the ancient Britons.[3] Bishop Davys is among those who expressly repudiated the view that the pagan Britons could be virtuous at all in the accepted sense. 'Some people may, perhaps, tell you that they were a very mild and gentle and harmless set of people; but don't believe a word of it. These good dispositions do not come naturally; they come from right education, and true religion; and, as these people had neither, you may depend upon it they were a very fierce and savage race.'[4] Other writers who particularly stressed the cruelty and barbarism of the pagan Britons included Mrs Trimmer, Charlotte Yonge, Milner and Symes, all of whom are writers with a markedly religious point of view.[5] However, horror at the actions of the Britons is not confined to this group. Pringle, who tended to display a practical rather than an idealistic attitude to historical events, described Druidism as 'the worst of all supersititions'.[6]

In contrast, the arrival of Christianity was welcomed warmly as 'the

---

[1] Baldwin (1812), p. 8.
[2] Rodwell (1853), p. 8.
[3] Gleig (1853), p. 4.
[4] Davys (1822), pp. 2–3.
[5] Trimmer (1849), p. 6; Tonge (1880), Book 2, p. 8; Milner (1853), p. 6 Symes (1899), p. 34.
[6] Pringle (1907), p. 6.

greatest boon that could be conferred on a nation'.[1] Christianity was not merely welcomed because it put an end to the 'superstitions' or 'idolatries' of the pagans, as they were termed. Some writers saw it as the beginning of true morality and civilisation.[2] As Kipling and Fletcher put it: 'Without religion there can be no good morals and without good morals the wisest laws are futile.'[3] Symes also noted a practical benefit from the adoption of Christianity: 'Then too the Christian English have very much more in common with the civilized world than the heathen English could ever have had.'[4] One writer even hailed the arrival of Christianity apparently on the grounds that it brought the female sex into prominence:

'Now rose and fell the Christian light
Through many still eventful years,
And through that age with lustre bright
Full many a female name appears.'[5]

Primitive paganism was, however, not the only threat to Christianity. The sophisticated threat of Islam had to be described by textbook authors when they dealt with the Crusades. In the earlier nineteenth century a comparatively tolerant climate of opinion prevailed. Baldwin commented on the fact that any nation forms an ill opinion of its enemies and went on to point out that, disregarding the evidence of Saracenic culture and learning, the people of the Middle Ages chose to depict 'a fierce looking face with enormous whiskers at the door of an inn and calling it the "Saracen's Head".'[6] Mrs Trimmer also allowed the infidel some virtues. To her, Saladin's generosity to the poor of every religion and his display of a shroud to remind himself and others of the fleeting nature of earthly triumph contrasted favourably with Richard I's vainglorious behaviour.[7] Another early textbook writer, Mrs Hack, was at pains to stress that Mohammed 'was no vulgar imposter'.[8]

Later in the nineteenth century, the tone hardened and in contrast a stereotype infidel Turk is depicted, whose dominant attribute is cruelty, but who is sometimes endowed with other vices too. A typical view was

---

[1] Collier (1875), p. 17.
[2] Markham (1874), p. 20.
[3] Fletcher and Kipling (1911), p. 231.
[4] Symes (1899), p. 34.
[5] Bourne (c. 1870), p. 11.
[6] Baldwin (1812), p. 44.
[7] Trimmer (1849), p. 65.
[8] Hack (1872 ed.), p. 89.

that: 'The hardships of the journey were greatly increased by the insults which the Christians received from the Moslems who plundered them of what they possessed and turned their worship to ridicule.'[1] Here the infidel is depicted as callous and dishonest as well as hostile in attitude to the Christian faith. A similar view was expressed by Miss Rodwell: 'But Jerusalem then belonged to the Turks who hated all Christians and treated them cruelly when they went there.'[2] The trait of cruelty was remarked on by the author of the *Cambridge Reader*[3] and other authors who went into a detailed account of how: 'the insults, robberies, extortions practised on the pilgrims who visited the Holy Sepulchre roused the indignation of all Christendom'.[4]

Opinions about the Crusades themselves and the motives and character of those who took part in them also underwent a change during the nineteenth century. One or two writers flatly denied that the Crusades could be justified on Christian principles. Mrs Markham wrote that: 'The Crusaders had no right to attack the infidels. It was, to say the least of it, a mad unjust war', and she added later: 'Enthusiasm can make people undertake anything.'[5] This example of a distinctly latitudinarian attitude to religious zeal is perhaps echoed by Hort, who remarked tolerantly that the Crusade 'was esteemed at that time a service highly acceptable to the Almighty'[6]—implying that his own age knew better. Writers who elsewhere show that they were themselves imbued with evangelical religious zeal also disapproved of the Crusades, however. Collier wrote: 'When I think of the Crusades, I never can help admiring the zeal and devotion of those who went forth in the cause of the Christian religion. At the same time I think they were mistaken in their notions of religion in expecting to propagate the mild spirit of the Christian faith by means of war and bloodshed.'[7] He went on to compare the enthusiasm of the Crusader with the indifference which he sees in the modern world, but he has acknowledged that, in principle at least, the Crusaders were wrong. This view is also shared by Milner, who did not consider the expeditions to the Holy Land to be 'altogether unprofitable', but who remarked on 'the grossly mistaken principles upon which these expeditions rested and the atrocities to which

---

[1] Murby (1895), p. 26.
[2] Rodwell (1853), p. 44.
[3] *Cambridge* (1911), vol. I, p. 56.
[4] Adams (1871), p. 9.
[5] Markham (1874), p. 96.
[6] Hort (1822), p. 94.
[7] Collier (1875), p. 77.

[98]

they led'.[1] This tendency to condemn in part the principles behind the Crusades while finding some practical advantages which accrued from them is also to be found in the Roman Catholic writer, Father Flanagan. In his booklet, the question is asked whether the wars were any use to England, and the reply is: 'Very little. They were a great burden upon the growing trade and commerce of the country, but they helped to bring down the great power of the king and his nobles.'[2]

The disregard of ethical discussions about the Crusades and the stress on their practical value is especially evident in opinions about Richard I himself. Like other martial leaders of the Middle Ages he was often condemned. Sometimes this condemnation was on moral grounds. Typical criticisms were that: 'He was fond of fighting for fighting's sake',[3] and 'turbulent person'.[4] Yet there was increasing emphasis on the purely practical disadvantages which Richard's absence on crusade brought to his country: 'He was indeed the model of a feudal knight but the King of England who spent six months among his people during a reign of ten years and whose highest victories brought poverty and hunger to English homes cannot but be deemed unworthy of the name.'[5] Those who praise Richard—and they are much in the minority—tend to do so because, for instance he went on a Crusade, 'so that dear England should be heard of all over the world'[6]— that is on practical and patriotic grounds. Possibly the increasingly pragmatic approach to such topics in textbooks of the later years of Victoria's reign reflects the waning influences of the evangelical movement and of religious zeal in general. Certainly sectarian feeling, though still strong, had somewhat abated, though its influence, especially on education, could not be disregarded.

The members of the Roman Catholic Church remained one of the most important and controversial minorities in Britain as a whole, although in Ireland they constituted a majority. In the years following the Reformation allegiance to the Pope had become linked with the tradition of disloyalty to the Crown in England. Moreover, Whig historians, by a process of 'guilt by association', identified Roman Catholicism with the 'losing' Stuart cause and Protestantism with the 'winning' Parliamentarian side in

---

[1] Milner (1855), p. 218.
[2] Flanagan (*c.* 1850), p. 26.
[3] Chambers (1885), p. 60.
[4] Hearnshaw (1914), p. 37.
[5] Collier (1875), p. 81.
[6] Callcott (1872), p. 67.

the struggles between King and Parliament in the seventeenth century. Protestantism therefore became to be considered libertarian and progressive in character, and Roman Catholicism to be thought reactionary and repressive. During the nineteenth century fear of Roman Catholicism was still evident in the opposition to the passing of Catholic Emancipation in 1829 and the return of the Catholic hierarchy to England in 1850. Likewise the association of Roman Catholicism with rebellion in Ireland also served to encourage popular suspicion of it in England and this continued to some extent into the twentieth century.

However, the same period also witnessed growing toleration between the Catholic and Protestant sides which showed itself in the freeing of the former from all political and religious disabilities within the law. Towards the end of the nineteenth century animosities between the various protestant sects also declined. The setting up of state schools was for long delayed by arguments as to the type of religious instruction and worship to be conducted in them. These ranged from assertions that the teaching of the Anglican Church should be paramount[1] to claims that there should be complete separation of education and religion.[2] However, by 1870 sectarian feeling had waned sufficiently for the Forster Act to be passed and to come into force without successful protest. Henceforth schools of the Anglican, Non-conformist and Roman Catholic denominations were aided impartially by the state, but were faced with rival Board Schools where non-denominational teaching prevailed.

In spite of the growing tolerance for Catholicism, the textbooks examined were overwhelmingly Protestant in character. Only Father Flanagan's catechism, Miss Drane's history and the books by Livesey published by Burns and Oates, are obviously by Catholic writers, although Farr does seem pro-Catholic at times and one or two writers claim to have made use of Lingard's history. Maunder, for instance, claimed. 'We have selected Lingard's account of this matter (the dissolution of the monasteries) because that historian has a very evident leaning to the Catholic side of every question of English history, and yet he, unconsciously perhaps, goes far towards justifying Henry's measures against the monkish superstitions and impostures, no matter what his motives may have been.'[3] Father Flanagan adopts a similar attitude when he takes his figure of 72,000

---

[1] *Remarks on the Objects of Public Education* (1828).
[2] *The Public 'Pearl'* (1854).
[3] Maunder (1864), p. 311.

victims during Henry VIII's reign from *Allison's Guide*.[1] On the whole, however, both sides remain fairly distinct in their treatment of events.

The anti-Catholic attitudes of most writers can be seen even in their treatment of the Saxon period. Augustine's missionary journey to the pagan Saxons was sometimes viewed with dismay because it brought England within the orbit of the Roman see. Baldwin described Augustine's work as 'teaching us ignorance',[2] and Mrs Trimmer painted a sour picture of the effect of his mission on the Christian faith in England which 'had become sadly corrupted by popery; a false faith, which, while it darkens men's understanding, corrupts their morals'.[3] In contrast, Father Flanagan naturally stressed the benefits of Augustine's mission and outlined the Catholic view of papal claims to rule the Church. In answer to the question whether St Peter was succeeded by anyone as head of the Church, the answer is given: 'Yes. The Popes, or bishops of Rome have come down, one after the other, from St Peter's time to the present day.'[4] Apart from Augustine, the other controversial figure in the Saxon Church is Dunstan. He had his defenders even among protestant writers, it is true. Gleig[5] and the author of *Allison's Guide* both praised him, referring to his 'great learning and scientific knowledge', in the case of the latter.[6] There was a tendency to compare Dunstan with Becket because of his alleged quarrel with King Edgar over his marriage to Queen Elfgiva. One author told a highly coloured and inaccurate story of this theme and concluded. 'How little was the spirit of the Gospel understood by an archbishop who could tacitly sanction such revolting cruelties.'[7] A common charge against Dunstan was his hypocrisy and supersition,[8] and this was repeated against other leaders of the Catholic Church, notably Becket. Miss Rodwell openly made the comparison, remarking of Becket that 'he grew so proud that he wanted to rule everything his own way as Dunstan did in the time of the Saxon Kings'.[9]

The attack on Becket seems, in fact, to have been based on a low view of his personal qualities or on his adherance to an alien power, the bishop of

---

[1] Flanagan (*c.* 1850), p. 29.
[2] Baldwin (1812), p. 15.
[3] Trimmer (1849), p. 24.
[4] Flanagan (*c.* 1850), p. 4.
[5] Gleig (1856), p. 37.
[6] *Allison* (1880), p. 51.
[7] Curtis (1875), p. 13.
[8] Hort (1822), p. 56.
[9] Rodwell (1853), p. 54.

Rome. Even Becket's religious exercises come under unsympathetic scrutiny. In one book there is a description of how he flogged himself and washed the feet of beggars every day. The question follows: 'Why was he so foolish and filthy?' to be followed by the answer: 'Because, like the ancient Pharisees he wanted to gain the applause of holy men and to be esteemed a very holy and mortified saint.'[1] Although some writers allowed him 'some religious feelings',[2] most echoed Bishop Davy's account of the Archbishop's character. 'But under his appearance of humility Becket had a heart full of pride and ambition. He had very great power among the clergy but instead of using it in support of the king, as a Christian subject ought to do, he employed it in opposition to his sovereign, and wished to have the clergy, a rich and powerful body, thinking more about their earthly dignity than their heavenly calling.'[3] The accusations of disloyalty to the King and treachery which are fairly common in all types of books[4] were most forcefully summed up by Fletcher: 'Much as Englishmen hated their tyrannical king, they hated still more the idea of an Italian priest dealing thus with the Crown and liberty of England.'[5] It seems likely, indeed, that it was not merely Becket's opposition to Henry II, but his allegiance to an alien power that disturbed so many writers.

Even accounts of his death show traces of the hostile opinions formed of him. Livesey, as might be expected, gave a sympathetic account,[6] and one or two other writers showed sympathy for the martyr. Symes, for instance, declared that: 'He met his death with a courage that won the admiration of all men.'[7] In contrast, a few writers at the other extreme succeed in making it look as if it was entirely Becket's own fault that he was murdered. One claimed that the knights did not intend to kill Becket, but were provoked by his hasty words,[8] and another author even made it look as if the Archbishop started the violence. 'As he uttered these words, the Archbishop seized Tracy by the surcoat and flung him back with such violence as to bring him almost to the ground. It was the act of a moment and in a moment it was terribly requited.'[9]

The medieval clergy in general came under attack with Becket, though

---

1 *Allison* (1880), p. 51.
2 Baldwin (1812), p. 39.
3 Davys (1822), p. 32.
4 Legge (1864), p. 74.
5 Fletcher and Kipling (1911), p. 72.
6 Livesay (1908), p. 47.
7 Symes (1899), p. 81.
8 1907, p. 18.
9 Gleig (1853), p. 87.

there are significant variations in descriptions of their conduct. At the beginning of the century Hort stated his objections to them, which appear to be based mainly on their superstitious beliefs and practices: 'They professed the faith of Christ without understanding its principles, and consequently without feeling its blessed influence. False miracles, pompous rites and ceremonies, the worship of saints and relics, expiation of the vilest sins by penance, by pilgrimages to Rome, or by rich gifts to the Church, were proposed to them and there, in great measure accorded with their credulous dispositions.'[1] Hort's view is essentially that of a man who believes that he lives in the age of reason. He feels that he must try to explain why, although the medieval Christians come under the influence of the truth faith, they apparently failed to understand it in the way which had been granted to less superstitious later generations. This attitude is shared by other writers, whose books were written at the end of the eighteenth century or the beginning of the nineteenth. Mrs Trimmer, for instance, remarked on the 'depth of superstition and mental slavery' into which the people of the Middle Ages had fallen.[2]

In contrast, later writers concentrated their attack not on the ignorance and superstititon of the clergy, but on their immorality. One asserted: 'The priests were shockingly corrupt and are charged with idleness, gluttony and drunkenness and adultery; yet they persecuted and put to death by the fagot those who exposed their bad practices.'[3] Other writers condemned the friars for their laziness in avoiding honest toil and living off alms,[4] or insinuated that there were 'many wicked men even thieves and murderers in the Church',[5] whom it protected from just punishment. The Catholic defence against these accusations is interesting in that it does not usually answer them directly, but instead paints a positive picture of the Church as the defence of the weak against the strong. Father Flanagan declared that 'it punished with excommunication some of the most powerful and bloodthirsty men in the country',[6] and Cobbett, whose history was influenced by Lingard's, painted a picture of the 'ease and happiness and harmony and Christian charity enjoyed so abundantly' under the aegis of the clergy in the Middle Ages.[7]

---

[1] Hort (1822), p. 27.
[2] Trimmer (1849), p. 75.
[3] Bullock (1861), p. 83.
[4] Callcott (1875), p. 145.
[5] *Jack* (1905), vol. II, p. 68.
[6] Flanagan (*c.* 1850), p. 4.
[7] Cobbett (1824), para. 2.

When we come to consider attitudes to the Reformation in England itself we find, of course, many general expressions of opinion in favour of the Protestant side. One came from a lecturer at the Borough Road Training College: 'It behoves us who enjoy the religious privileges which have been under the divine blessing preserved from the time of the Reformation, to exhibit devout gratitude for the boon. . . . We should use our influence in guiding others into the true path . . . so that the millenium should come.'[1] Other writers praised Luther for exposing 'the error of the Church of Rome'[2] or commented on the greater opportunities for reading the Bible which were granted after the Reformation: 'But now a book was placed in everyman's hand which he could read for himself, and by which he could direct his life and opinions.'[3] There are also expressions which suggest that nationalist bias enters into discussion of the Reformation. The author of *Cassells History*, for instance, declared that: 'Elizabeth was quite determined not to allow the Pope or anybody else to meddle in any English business.'[4]

On the other hand, the expressions of opinion about the Catholic martyr More do show that on the whole he emerges as most writers' idea of the perfect religious hero, just as Alfred emerges as the perfect moral hero. He was described as 'one of the most amiable and virtuous men that ever lived',[5] and 'the most perfect and spotless character that ever graced the English dominions'.[6] Lady Callcott declared: 'As long as there are good people in the world, Sir Thomas More and his daughter will be loved wherever their name are heard'.[7] and Gleig, staunchly protestant though he is, admitted: 'His conscience was too pure to admit equivocation, though the reward of equivocating ever so slightly would have been not less than life.'[8] Few writers commented on the lighter side of More's character, though one described him as 'witty, truthful and noble-hearted'.[9] More is accepted not only for the excellence of his character and his courage in the face of danger, but even for his devotion to his religion which many of the writers have already asserted is a deluded one. Thus the author of the

---

1 Curtis (1860), pp. 162–3.
2 Pringle (1907), p. 62.
3 *Cassells* (1883), p. 199.
4 *Cassells, Stories from English History* (1884), p. 117.
5 *Allison* (1880), p. 79.
6 Baldwin (1812), p. 92.
7 Callcott (1872), p. 155.
8 Gleig (1856), p. 211.
9 *Cassells* (1883), p. 196.

Chambers Reader sympathetically described how 'More was a good man. He had been brought up in the old religion and lived it',[1] and Farr, showing indignation at the way in which More was beheaded for his failure to accept the first Act of Supremacy, added: 'These murders spread a panic throughout the nation: and in all foreign countries where civilization had made any progress they excited universal execration.'[2] Farr is one of those who go on to suggest that Henry VIII's savage measures against More and others were necessary to succeed in 'shaking off the degrading domination of the see of Rome'[3] and others also justified the action against More on the grounds of national emergency.[4] No one, however, actually attacks his character and motives, though some writers, such as the author of the *Blackwoods Reader*, described his sufferings in strictly unemotional terms.[5]

It is perhaps surprising to find that attitudes to monasticism at the time of the dissolution, while not by any means so generally favourable as those with regard to More, are still sympathetic in a majority of writers. One of the more neutral views was that: 'Monasteries are large houses full of monks and nuns, people who have taken a vow never to marry, and to spend all their lives in saying their prayers and reading good books.'[6] A number of writers stressed the useful work for society which the monks performed. This included the establishment of schools, hospitality for the traveller and medical care and food for the poor.[7] Father Flanagan, as we might expect, made the fullest defence of the monks who, he says, tried to live as they would wish to die.[8] Later, when describing the Dissolution he also stressed the social usefulness of the monasteries: 'For there were neither poor-laws nor union-houses, nor any want of them, till the monasteries were destroyed.'[9]

Some writers, not necessarily favourable to monasticism itself, opposed the Dissolution because of what they hold to be Henry's cruelty and the rapacity of those who wished to take over monastic lands and wealth. Gleig, for instance, claimed: 'There can be no doubt that the crimes of the monastic orders were numerous, and that the frauds which they practised

---

[1] *Chambers* (1901–4), vol. 3, p. 64.
[2] Farr (1856), p. 233.
[3] Ibid. p. 238.
[4] Bright (1875), p. 395.
[5] *Blackwoods* (1883), vol. 2, pp. 172–3.
[6] Baldwin (1812), p. 16.
[7] *Allison* (1880), p. 95.
[8] Flanagan (*c.* 1860), p. 11.
[9] Flanagan (*c.* 1850), pp. 31–2.

in order to keep the people in ignorance and mental slavery merited not only exposure but punishment. Probably, too, the aggregate wealth of the clergy was exorbitant, but the violence which characterised the proceedings of the Reformers, their boundless rapacity, and utter disregard of the custom of the ages, proved more fatal to public morals, at least for the time, than all the vices of the condemned ecclesiastics.'[1] Gardiner, who described the Dissolution as 'an excuse for plundering',[2] and Littlewood are among those who stressed the idea that the desire for easy money and not horror at the vices of the monks was the real motive behind the Dissolution.[3]

On the other hand, there are some writers, a sizeable number, though not a majority, for whom the condition of the monasteries justified all action taken against them. One, for instance, remarked that 'a mistaken piety had produced in Italy a new species of monks called Benedictines who excluded themselves entirely from the world, renounced all claim to liberty and made a merit of the most inviolable chastity'.[4] This feeling that there was something unnatural in monastic life is echoed in other writers, notably Fletcher, who saw the monks as evading their military and other responsibilities. 'But this meant you neglected your worldly duties, such as defending your country, tilling your fields, providing for your wife and children.'[5] Other writers attacked the crimes of the monks rather than the ideal of monasticism itself. Monasteries were variously described as 'dens of vice rather than abodes of virtue'[6] and as 'hotbeds of vice and superstition',[7] and reference was made to their excessive wealth as well as their scandalous moral condition.[8]

The persecution of protestants in Mary's reign calls forth even more stridently protestant attitudes in the majority of writers. Many of them had strong moral objections to the cruelty and killing associated with religious persecution and they tended to dwell on this aspect of Mary's policy rather than on the dangers of Catholicism itself. It is the Queen's alleged bigotry rather than her actual beliefs which concern them: 'Instead of branding her with the name of 'Bloody Mary'', we should rather pity the

---

[1] Gleig (1856), p. 211.
[2] Gardiner (1888), pp. 91–2.
[3] Littlewood (1869), p. 75.
[4] Hume (1875), p. 49.
[5] Fletcher and Kipling (1911), p. 35.
[6] Bartle (1865), p. 202.
[7] Bullock (1861), p. 99.
[8] Conan and Kendall (1902), p. 200.

Queen who in her religious zeal forgot the mercy natural to a woman and who saw before she died every aim and hope of her life baffled and broken.'[1] Some writers viewed the persecution more in its religious context as providing the triumph of protestantism through the sufferings of martyrs. Sometimes the accounts of the persecutions were highly coloured: 'There the stake and the fagot were in almost constant use, and the dwellings round were lighted up by the red glare of the fires which were adding so many to the "noble army of martyrs".'[2] On the whole, Cranmer, the most important of those who were executed for their faith in Mary's reign, was not well regarded because of his doubts and hesitations. One writer admitted somewhat grudgingly: 'Thus by a noble death he atoned for his cowardly compliance in the wicked designs of his superior during life.'[3] In some textbooks there are more restrained accounts of Mary's reign. Lady Callcott remarked: 'However, in England there were a great many good men on both sides',[4] and Miss Rodwell avoided giving too many details of the persecution: 'I will not say much about these dreadful things, though I must not be quite silent about them or you would not know how much cause you have to be thankful that you live in better times.'[5] Comparatively mild as it is, her comment helps to explain some of the impetus behind the religious attitudes of protestant writers about the Reformation. They seem to have written with the design, conscious and unconscious, of suggesting to their readers that as in politics, so in religion, the calm of the present *status quo* was better than the turbulence of past disorder.

Catholic writers, it is interesting to note, adopted much the same tactics as their opponents. Livesey, for instance, while defending the 'absolute sincerity and simpleness of heart'[6] of Mary, attacked the character of Cranmer and his master, Henry VIII, even comparing the latter to Ahab in that the dogs licked his blood after his death.[7] Livesey also referred to the Archbishop's 'elastic conscience'[8] and far from lamenting his death, remarked: 'So in flames and smoke, disappeared the least revered figure of a corrupt generation.'[9] In contrast he devoted several chapters to the

---

[1] Collier (1875), p. 173.
[2] Clough (*c.* 1870), p. 55.
[3] *Cassells* (1883), p. 216.
[4] Callcott (1875), p. 148.
[5] Rodwell (1853), p. 138.
[6] Livesey (1908), p. 99.
[7] Ibid. p. 94.
[8] *Granville* (1885), vol. 2, p. 89.
[9] Ibid. p. 97.

sufferings of Catherine of Aragon and Thomas More and explained More's stand: 'For if it be lawful to reject the authority of the Vicar of Christ, it may be pleaded that it is lawful also to deny any other doctrine of the Catholic Church.'[1] Both Livesey and Father Flanagan drew attention to the Catholic martyrs of Elizabeth's reign which, with the exception of Mary, Queen of Scots, the protestant writers almost entirely omit. Father Flanagan, for instance, devoted five pages in a very small book of fifty-six, to a criticism of Elizabeth's religious policy.

When dealing with the Stuart period, the writers were more concerned with political rather than religious affairs, and in fact it is the Catholic writers who refer to incidents which affected their own position during the seventeenth century and the protestant writers who tend to pass them over in silence. The Gunpowder Plot, for instance, receives surprisingly little attention. It is true that a few writers referred to the 'dreadful scene'[2] or the 'horrid plan'.[3] However, most writers described it in unemotional terms where it is mentioned at all, and Conan and Kendall stressed the horrible tortures endured by Guido Fawkes by describing the difference between his signature before and after torture.[4] In contrast, Livesey and Father Flanagan devoted some time to exonerating the majority of Catholics from such a heinous design. The former poses the question: 'Did not the great body of Catholics show their liking for the gunpowder plot?' and gives the answer: 'Never. They did not so much as know that such a wicked thing was going on.'[5] Later, Father Flanagan noted the loyalty shown by the Catholics during the Civil War, and in answer to a question whether the Catholics still remained faithful to the king who had persecuted them, replied that 'they fought for him to the last and they saved his son, afterwards Charles II, when the Puritans were hunting him down in Staffordshire'.[6]

The Popish Plot which occurred after Charles II's restoration and which resulted in the victimisation of many innocent Catholics on the false evidence of Titus Oates, is an aspect of the past which goes strangely unnoticed by protestant writers. At the beginning of the century Baldwin admitted it to be 'one of the most wicked things we read of in history'.[7]

---

1 *Granville* (1885), Vol. 1, p. 93.
2 Morris (1883), p. 5.
3 Ransome (1890), p. 129.
4 Conan and Kendall (1902), p. 256.
5 Flanagan (*c.* 1850), p. 44.
6 Ibid. p. 46.
7 Baldwin (1812), p. 118.

Later there was the occasional attempt at a defence: 'It was not perhaps unnatural in the protestant people of England to attach a portion of the guilt of a purely popish conspiracy to the whole body of papists throughout the kingdom.'[1] Generally the Popish plot was glossed over, however. In contrast, a considerable number of writers find time to comment on the conversion to Catholicism of Charles II. The author of the *History of England Mostly in Words of One Syllable,* for instance, remarked: 'When this came to be known, men were shocked and grieved, and the loss of such a king did not seem great.[2] Most writers were, of course, in favour of the 1688 Revolution on political grounds, but there is little doubt that considerations of a religious character also played their part. One author commented—of the flight of James II: 'Thus was England freed from the power of a persecuting bigot.'[3]

In accounts of more recent times, anti-Catholic bias is again shown in the neglect of such incidents discreditable to the Protestant cause as the anti-Catholic Gordon riots. The only writer who devoted much space to recounting them is the Catholic Livesey, who remarked: 'Our countrymen disgraced themselves sadly at home.'[4] On the other hand, the emancipation of Catholics from the legal impediments to taking a full part in public life, was generally welcomed, except by a few writers of the earlier nineteenth century who obviously felt personally affected by the controversy. One remarked that Wellington was regarded as the betrayer of his country over Catholic Emancipation,[5] another stressed that it was passed with 'great reluctance',[6] and to another it seemed to some to be 'replete with danger to the protestant majority of the country'.[7] On the other hand, writers later in the century are wholeheartedly in favour of the change. Collier remarked that 'most grievous laws had been pressing on our Roman Catholic fellow subjects with appalling severity'[8] and the author of an elementary school reader stated bluntly: 'Thus a piece of injustice that was a standing disgrace to England was swept away.'[9] Miss Yonge likewise admitted the justice of the reform in Ireland: 'Since so many Irish were

---

[1] Gleig (1856), p. 306.
[2] 1907, p. 66.
[3] Farr (1856), p. 337.
[4] *Granville* (1902), pp. 158–60.
[5] Cooper (1843), p. 202.
[6] Trimmer (1849), p. 340.
[7] Maunder (1864), p. 486.
[8] Collier (1869), p. 47.
[9] *Tower* (1911), p. 122.

Romanists it was not fair that they should have no voice in the government.'[1] Pro-Catholic writers naturally welcomed the change, though McCarthy comments on the way in which its further development was delayed by royal opposition: 'It would be unjust and even cruel to deny that the king (William IV) was a religious man according to his lights but his lights were many times blurred by sundry conditions.'[2] On one point only is there controversy in the text-books about another event in recent times. Some writers expressed dismay at the return of the Catholic hierarchy to England on the orders of Pius IX. One noted his 'imperious language'[3] and another commented on the strength of opposition to the step.[4] In contrast, the Catholic writer, Livesey, devoted some effort to explaining what the return of the hierarchy actually meant.[5]

Differing attitudes to events within the Protestant sects are not always easy to discern. The influence of the Evangelical Movement can be detected in the greater emphasis on moral considerations noted above and in occasional notes or praise for those who encouraged Bible reading. It may be suspected that textbooks which give favourable mention to Wesley and Whitfield were written by Methodists, but this is impossible to prove given the anonymity or obscurity of many of the textbook writers. It is easier to detect one section of opinion within the Church of England itself. The Clapham sect evangelicals like the latitudinarians before them had shared many of their beliefs with protestant dissenters of all sects. However, the Church had been clearly distinguished from the latter by its privileged position in law. After the repeat of the Test and Corporation Acts of 1828 dissenters were gradually freed from their disabilities. The members of the Tractarian or Oxford Movement responded by finding new grounds of difference between the Church of England and the protestant dissenters. They stressed salvation by grace which came through the sacraments only administered by clergy who had been duly ordained by bishops of the Church. The influence of the Oxford Movement was seen in a revival of loyalty to the Church of England as part of the ancient Catholic Church, and an interest in ceremonies and beliefs which had been rejected at the time of the Reformation. One writer whose religious background is known to us, Charlotte M. Yonge, was in fact criticised for propagating

---

[1] Yonge (1880), vol. 5, p. 234.
[2] McCarthy (1899), p. 45.
[3] Farr and Scott (1861), p. 467.
[4] Beale (1858), p. 142.
[5] *Granville* (1908), p. 166.

these 'High Church' views.[1] On the whole, however, religious opinions in her work do not seem to differ significantly from those of other writers of the period, except for an occasional reference to the belief that the Church of England was still part of the Catholic Church.[2] Nor does that of her friend, Eleanor Sewell, who was also a supporter of the Oxford Movement. There exists, however, one very curious work which claimed to give a churchman's view of English history to children and so 'to secure a correct first impression in their minds'.[3] In many respects the author merely followed the opinions of the Roman Catholic party, detesting Henry VIII and Elizabeth I, while defending Mary. However, he shows his Anglo-Catholic sentiments when he remarks in the 'remarkable improvement' in the Church of England at the period of the Oxford Movement.[4] This is confirmed by his definition of 'protestant' as erroneously applied to those who believe that every man should obey the Bible according to his own interpretation. He added. 'Our Church never was, nor is, Protestant in the former sense: it is true that churchmen sometimes call themselves Protestants, but they only mean today that they are not now in communion with the Church of Rome.'[5] This author was perhaps unusual in the way in which he acknowledged his task as a religious propagandist and pursued it so obviously, but his opinions are only marginally more extreme than those to be found in books for middle-class schools and elementary school readers whose authors made no special claims to be representatives of any church.

These expressions of sectarian feeling, striking as they are, seem to be significant because they give so misleading a picture of the changes in the religious life of England. To read them one might suppose that religious fervour contained unabated until 1914, that no influential and respectable voices had ever been raised against Christianity, that the mass of the working population were committed churchgoers whose main preoccupation was the shortcomings of the Church of Rome. Certainly many of these features, especially the last, were much in evidence in Victorian England, but it was also an age of acute crisis of belief. Neither this uncertainty not the other equally great doubt about Britain's ability to maintain her position in the world ever found its way into history textbooks.

---

[1] *Educational Times* (1 Dec. 1879), p. 357.
[2] See above p. 192.
[3] *English History for Children* (1845), preface.
[4] Ibid. p. 291.
[5] Ibid. p. 154.

CHAPTER V

Opinions about England and her Place in the World

'. . . However obscurely born, he may be excused for
being proud that he is an Englishman.'[1]

ELIGION, politics and patriotism often seemed inseparable in Victorian
England. Writers compared the state of religious and civil liberty
attained in England with that elsewhere and concluded that the
English were uniquely blessed by providence. One writer, in the *Educational Times*, it is true, had to admit that the United States of America
seemed to be on the right road. Nevertheless she had not existed long
enough for any definite judgment to be made.[2] Granted such opinions, it is
not surprising that they were thought important enough to teach the
younger generation, and not surprising that this aspect of history textbooks had drawn so much attention since.[3] The growth of movements for
international understanding and the decline of English power and prestige
have combined to make such sentiments both odious and ridiculous. Yet a
closer examination of the variety of opinions which history textbooks of
the period 1800–1914 actually contained suggest that such reactions are not
always justified. They show that there were differing interpretations of
patriotism, various views of other races and of Britain's imperial rule. The
predominating views change drastically in conformity with contemporary
opinion, but they were rarely left unchallenged by other writers who
disputed them.

In the early years of the nineteenth century the connection between the
teaching of history and patriotism was not overlooked, but stress was laid
on the positive aspect of patriotism, namely, love of country, rather on the
negative aspects which include dislike and fear of other nations. Priestley
wrote at the end of the eighteenth century that: 'History frees the mind
from many prejudices, and particularly national prejudices: but will confirm the attachment of a Briton to his country.'[4] This moderate attitude

---

[1] Ross (1872), p. 76.
[2] Sept. 1855, p. 205.
[3] Notably in E. H. Dance's *History the Betrayer*.
[4] *Miscellaneous Observations Concerning Education* (1812 ed.), p. 205.

can be traced right through the period. It is present, for instance, in J. G. Fitch's description of the duty of the history teacher. He wrote: 'Nor ought we to overlook the necessity for so teaching as to inspire our scholars with a love and admiration of the country we live in and for the institutions by which we are governed. . . . But after all patriotism is one of the things which our teaching ought to cultivate—a rational and affectionate regard for the country in which we are born, and for the privileges we enjoy in it.'[1] Even during the period of international tension which culminated in the First World War a substantial number of writers clung to these views. For instance, in 1911 an L.C.C. Report on the teaching of history remarked on the way in which patriotism was taught in other European countries, notably France and Germany—and concluded that to teach history with so definite a purpose was not 'advisable or successful even from the point of view adopted'.[2] A little later J. Headlam, writing on 'The Effect of the War on the Teaching of History' remarked that to teach history with a strong nationalistic bias was unacceptable 'not because it is too patriotic, but because it is unworthy and, according to our views, really antipatriotic'.[3] In the same periodical, C. H. K. Marten called for 'intelligent, but not blind patriotism'.[4]

However, Fitch, Marten, Headlam and their like were forced to state their views so boldly because by the end of the second half of the nineteenth century there had emerged a vociferous group which approved the teaching of history so as to encourage extreme forms of patriotism in the child. The *Educational Times* for 1 November 1900 contained the report of a lecture on the 'Teaching of Patriotism' by J. J. Findlay which describes the teaching of history for this purpose in America and Germany and goes on to assert: 'Now ten years ago, if we had cited these two nations as examples for Great Britain to imitate we should certainly have been reminded that the same need does not exist among ourselves. . . . But today no one will consider the discussion as unsuitable.'[5] In the ensuing discussion J. G. Fitch vehemently took issue with the speaker and far from seeing the value of 'flag-saving' blamed it for much of the violence then current in society.[6] However, there is an obvious connection between the hatred and

---

[1] *Lectures on Teaching* (1885), p. 392.
[2] *Report on the Teaching of History*, p. 16.
[3] *History* (1918), p. 16.
[4] *History* (1913), p. 98.
[5] *Educational Times* (1900), p. 42.
[6] Ibid.

fear of foreign powers which touched Britain in the years before 1914 and
the increased stress on the need for the teaching of devotion to country. In
what appears to be a reply to Headlam's article, W. H. Webb wrote angrily
that patriotism 'the twin sister of history' was ignored by the school code.
He contrasted this unfavourably with the system of Germany, Japan and
the Balkans. 'The children of those countries imbibed the love of country
with their mother's milk, and when they grow older, History and Patriotism
took their hands and guided them into the paths any true lover of his own
land ought to go.'[1] Although some private individuals and institutions were
undertaking what ought to be a government duty, the whole Empire was
suffering from the neglect of patriotism in history teaching, Webb believed.
There is some slight evidence that reviewers of history textbooks were
eager to praise authors who were notably patriotic in their attitudes towards
the end of the nineteenth century. One dealing with Curtis's *History*
commented: 'It is no light matter to animate the rising youth of England
with a spirit of dignified pride in the great traditions of a glorious past
and a noble future which is ours.'[2] Chambers' *Short History of England*
was commended for its 'national tone',[3] and the *Nelson History Reader*
'Victoria the Great' was praised as 'likely to aid in producing a feeling of
loyalty and patriotism among the young'.[4] The influence of reviewers in
encouraging the more patriotically inclined textbooks must not be over-
stressed, however. The *Educational Times*—by no means a radical periodical—contained an extremely hostile review of the school history by
Rudyard Kipling and C. R. L. Fletcher which is heavily tinged with a
nationalistic bias. The reviewer commented on Fletcher's 'inconsistency
and crudeness of political thought' and noted that while the author dis-
claims the intention to guide the pupil's opinions, 'he still continues to try'.
With reference to his 'imperialist judgments', he concluded: 'He is un-
controllable and irresponsible—the Puck of historians. Mr Kipling
poetises well with rough vigour on the imperial note. The book needs to be
revised in a serious spirit.'[5]

Whatever form their patriotism took, however, most writers had an
exalted view of Britain's achievements and place in the world. Such a view
was by no means confined to the nineteenth century. Lord Chesterfield, for

---

[1] *History* (1913), p. 53.
[2] *School Board Chronicle* (1877), p. 58.
[3] *Educational Times* (1 Nov. 1880), p. 285.
[4] Ibid. (1897), p. 465.
[5] *Educational Times* (1912), p. 136.

instance, wrote to his son with pride that 'our fleets and armies are numerous and valiant, and, when well-directed, always victorious; the latter have distinguished themselves in every quarter of the globe . . . while the former have borne the English name and flag triumphant from the frozen regions of the North to the Antarctic circle'.[1] However, the advance of British power and prestige after the Napoleonic Wars, based as they were on industrial and economic strength, served to increase belief in the good fortune and superiority over others of the British race. At the opening of the Great Exhibition of 1851, the Archbishop of Canterbury expressed his joy that other nations were assembled to admire the triumphs of British industry and art, linking these firmly with the approval and assistance of the Almighty.[2] By the end of the century the growth of the Empire in Africa and elsewhere had reinforced complacency about Britain's position, although there were incipient fears that she was being challenged by Germany and other growing powers.[3] Sometimes the nationalism which occurred in various countries at the turn of the century was accompanied by rudimentary ideas of racial superiority. Such ideas were expressed in extreme form by the British politicians of the time, notably by Joseph Chamberlain who, in a public speech, declared: 'I believe in this race, the greatest governing race the world has ever seen; in this Anglo-Saxon race, so proud reaching, self-confident and determined, this race, which neither climate nor change can degenerate, which will infallibly be the predominant force of future history and universal civilisation.'[4] Certainly the views of Chamberlain and others who took an unusually exalted view of the nation's progress did not pass unchallenged. In politics Gladstone urged moderation and he was supported by those who were realistic towards Britain's achievements. In *Essays of a Birmingham Manufacturer*, W. L. Sargant pleaded that children should learn more of the history and achievements of other nations. He went on: 'It is not true, as some have maintained, that our literature is the best in the world. . . , and still less is it true that our Empire, politically and socially speaking, is the greatest that ever existed.'[5] Nevertheless, it must be admitted that Sargant was stating a minority view, although one which continued to be expressed even when the trend towards imperialism was at its height.

---

[1] *Letters from a Nobleman to his Son* (1810 ed.), p. 327.
[2] Quoted in *Ideas and Beliefs of the Victorians* (1949), p. 55.
[3] See earlier, p. 113.
[4] Quoted in *Ideas and Beliefs of the Victorians* (1949), pp. 329–30.
[5] (1870), p. 274.

Indeed, few of the writers whose textbooks were examined had any doubt about Britain's teaching place in the world. A typical view of the mid-nineteenth century was that: 'In reviewing this latter portion of our history we find many reasons for gratitude towards the Almighty Dispenser of events. The spirit of improvement which is abroad is pervading, as we have seen, not only our commerce, our manufactures, our means of communication, our agriculture, our literature, our science and art, but also our plans for the spiritual welfare of the rising generation and that of the world at large.'[1] The writer took it as the will of God that Britain should have made such progress in all those fields and regards her as the means of enlightenment (through the Christian message) for the rest of the world. Others took a rather more materialistic attitude. One clergyman wrote that: 'England is now a world-renowned country with unsurpassed monuments of industry and evidences of wealth, waving a flag in every accessible sea, extending an influence to every known political body, which her customs, her language, and her products are diffused over the face of the habitable earth.'[2] An even more purely commercial view was that: 'Our open markets together with the skill and industrial energy of the people, have had the effect of greatly benefitting the native shipping interest so much so that the commerce of the world is chiefly carried on in ships sailing under the British flag.'[3] It is instructive to compare these opinions, which date from the time when Britain's overseas Empire and trade were making vast strides, with the attitude of Hort earlier in the century. He attributed England's advanced position in the world to the interest of the Almighty, whom he termed the 'Supreme Moral Governor'. However, he based her claim to primacy in the world not on her success in commerce and conquest, but on her freedom from ignorant superstition and violence.[4] Thus although writers throughout the century generally agreed in praising their own country before all others, they would not all perhaps have accepted this somewhat boastful description of England in the year of Queen Victoria's Jubilee. 'Costly gifts and loyal addresses poured in upon Her Majesty and even from the most distant parts of the Empire, and foreign courts vied with each other in the warmth of their congratulations. Noble institutions were established to commemorate a reign, the most wonderful perhaps the world has yet seen.'[5]

---

[1] Gleig (1853), p. 624.
[2] Milner (1854), p. 1.
[3] Morris (1883), p. 255.
[4] Hort (1822), p. 210.
[5] *Collins* (1890), p. 266.

It is notable, however, that some writers who stressed Britain's leading position in the world also emphasised her moral and religious duties. For the writer of the early nineteenth century, power and prestige were often conditional on good conduct. Hort added a word of warning to his remarks on the greatness of the English nation: 'May Britons merit the continuance of those blessings by being a virtuous, moral and religious people, a people whose God is the Lord.'[1] His view is echoed in other textbooks of the period. Mrs Trimmer, for instance, concluded her history: 'Having a true love of your native land, you will be led to contribute your part towards its prosperity by practising that righteousness which alone EXALTETH A NATION.'[2] Mrs Markham also associated Henry V's success against the French with the evil conduct of the latter. 'The French people had at that period of their history arrived at a very dreadful pitch of wickedness and nothing, I think, appears more clear than that Henry was an especial instrument in the hands of Providence to humiliate and chastise them.'[3]

In later years it became less usual for writers to associate divine approval or otherwise with England's position in the world. However, the idea lingered on in the form of the feeling that power entailed certain moral duties. This received clear expression in the work of Lady Callcott. At first sight her statement that 'To teach the love of our country is almost a religious duty' appears surprising to a modern reader. However, she goes on: 'Let no man fear that to cultivate patriotism is to make men illiberal in feeling towards mankind in general. Is any man a worse citizen for being a good son or brother or father or husband? I am indeed persuaded that the well-grounded love of our own country is the best security for that enlightened philanthropy which is aimed at the perfection of moral education.' Something of what Lady Callcott meant by the last phrase is perhaps conveyed by her satisfaction that England had been able to keep out of most of the wars abroad in her day 'except to send help to the wounded soldiers and starving people'.[4] This idealised picture of Britain's role in the world nevertheless probably reflects what Lady Callcott thought it should be. The author of *Cassells Simple Outline* also stressed that nations must always treat each other and act justly because if they do not they 'have nearly always to suffer for it themselves in the end',[5] and seems to link this implicitly with England's success in the past—'. . . the more our

---

[1] Hort (1822), p. 4.
[2] Trimmer (1849), p. 393.
[3] Markham (1874), p. 185.
[4] Callcott (1872), p. 266.
[5] *Cassells Simple Outline* (1884) p. 181.

country has grown stronger and better, the more its rulers and its people have striven to act rightly. It is the duty of Englishmen to do their best to make England great in the future.' Thus although the rising generation was often given a grandiose conception of England's power, it was a power which entailed serious responsibilities and duties.

So much for England; but what of the nature of the Englishman? Another feature of the textbooks produced in the later years of Victoria's reign is the way in which they reflect the growing emphasis on racial characteristics which was a feature of the time. This was comparatively rare in the early nineteenth century. Indeed, Baldwin specifically ridicules those who 'contract an ill opinion' of nations with whom they happen to be at war and endow them with all manner of unpleasing characteristics.[1] It is, therefore, instructive to trace the idea of the 'typical Englishman' as he appears in the textbooks and compare him with the stereotype of other nations and races.

The Englishman is of course brave and honest. One writer asserted that 'You must be truthful if you would be truly English',[2] and another wrote. 'They all show the bold, frank, sturdy character which so strongly marks the Anglo-Saxon race.'[3] He later added: 'The English are the best sailors in the world partly because they are active, hardy and silent, and partly because they live in an island and are accustomed to the sea.'[4] This association of the British sailor with bravery and honesty can be traced back to Mrs Markham. At one point in her narrative little George remarks: 'No English seaman was ever disgraced, I'm sure', and his mother replies: 'I will grant you that very few have been so.'[5] Lord Palmerston was also seen in some books as exemplifying the best qualities of the Englishman. Gardiner described him as 'cheery, high spirited and worthily representing the race to which he belonged'.[6] It is interesting that the virtues of courage, cheerfulness and calmness in the face of danger, which are so often attributed to the typical Englishman are linked very closely with the Anglo-Saxon race in some books. Fletcher provides an extreme but not untypical view: 'The Saxon Englishman was a savage with the vices and cruelties of an overgrown schoolboy, a drunkard, a gambler and

---

[1] Baldwin (1812), p. 44.
[2] Laurie (1866), p. 266.
[3] *Granville* (1902), p. 121.
[4] Ibid, p. 156.
[5] Markham (1874), p. 427.
[6] Gardiner (1891), p. 960.

very stupid. But he was a truth-teller, a brave, patient and cool-headed fellow.'[1] Most writers are less keen on the Normans who are shown as cruel conquerors on the whole whose only virtue was that they were soon absorbed into the English nation. As Miss Rodwell put it somewhat whimsically: 'Jane: Ah I see now how it was that the Normans turned to English without any fairy at all. Mama: Yes Jane, time was the fairy and a good fairy too.'[2] Maunder is one of the few writers who endow the Englishman with anything approaching intellectual quality by comparing England's achievements with those of ancient Greece and Rome.[3] This is only an implied reference to intelligence, however, and it is perhaps significant that this is not a quality which writers generally felt able to attribute to the English. However, they are occasionally seen as religious and moral, in, for instance, the work of the athiest Ross.[4] He admitted that 'there must be something in *race* after all' and went on to express a typical view that 'however obscurely born, he may be excused for being proud that he is an Englishman'.[5] In fact Ross was born a Scot.

It is instructive to see how far other nations were shown to possess characteristics which would allow them to feel a similar pride in their race. Of the other races in the British Isles the Scots emerge as the most favoured nation, perhaps because they had never actually been conquered by the English. It is true that they are described as mean occasionally. Lady Callcott recalled with horror the way in which Charles I was handed over to the Parliamentarians by them: 'You will hardly believe, however, that those mean Scots actually sold the King to the English Parliament, but they did so.'[6] Nevertheless, they are considered brave and independent. Gardiner (himself a Scot) explained their attitude to Edward I's attempt to subdue them sympathetically, saying that what they wanted was to be 'ruled by a man of their own country and not by a foreigner'.[7] Moreover, Wallace appears as a much admired figure in nearly all textbooks. Where mentioned, he is the 'hero of Scottish freedom'[8] and we read of his 'noble acts' and how Edward tried to terrorise the Scottish people by putting him to a cruel death, but how it 'only made the Scots the more ready to fight

---

[1] Fletcher and Kipling (1911), p. 29.
[2] Rodwell (1853), p. 52.
[3] Maunder (1864), preface p. vi.
[4] Ross (1872), pp. 74–5.
[5] Ibid. p. 76.
[6] Callcott (1872), p. 203.
[7] Gardiner (1888), p. 57.
[8] *Cambridge* (1911), p. 58.

for the freedom of their country'.¹ So great was the admiration for Wallace, the Scottish patriot, that as early as April 1831 there was a protest in the *Quarterly Journal of Education* that one who was guilty of such barbarous conduct should be so praised. The reviewer believed that a more moderate view should be expressed. 'The cruelties of Wallace belong to the barbarous character of the age which he lived in, but that his noble spirit was his own.' Mrs Hack's history was considered too uncritical of him to be a good moral influence on the younger generation.²

In contrast the Welsh and the Irish are not so favourably treated as the Scots. The Welsh do not receive much attention at all, except at the time of their conquest by Edward I. Here there is some sympathy for them from Miss Rodwell, for instance, who remarked: 'This war was a sad pity and I am sorry to say Edward did many more things to grieve the poor Welsh people, who now had no king of their own to care for them.'³ The Irish too have a fair measure of sympathy from admirers through the nineteenth century. Of course, we would expect to find Father Flanagan and Justin McCarthy writing in their favour but it is surprising to find the author of *Allison's Guide* answering the question: 'Why did the Irish hate the English?' with a blunt 'Because they were so shamefully treated by them'.⁴ The same writer also stressed the greater learning and civilisation of Ireland in the past: 'It was much more civilised than England in the times of the Anglo-Saxons, and had many more learned men.'⁵ Elsewhere there are sympathetic references to the 'barbarous policy' of Cromwell in Ireland,⁶ and to Ireland's flirtation with France during the Napoleonic wars: 'Such a spirit of discontent was a warning to the protestant ruling class that there was a limit to the endurance of even the most oppressed people.'⁷ It is notable that most writers who are sympathetic to Ireland unconsciously convey the impression that the Irish need to be protected and thus that they are incapable of taking care of themselves.

This view is also implicit in the attitude of those hostile to Ireland, except that they add that the Irish are ungrateful for the help which is given to them. Farr, for instance, described the measures taken to help the

---

1 *Cambridge* (1911), p. 74.
2 April 1831, p. 385.
3 Rodwell (1853), p. 71.
4 *Allison* (1880), pp. 145–6.
5 Ibid.
6 Hume (1875), p. 442.
7 Morris (1883), p. 138.

Irish during the famine of 1845–6 (in which over a million people died): The hand of charity was willingly stretched forth in England for their relief; government and the nation united in aiding that unhappy people; and but for the timely aid afforded, the whole country would have been one vast scene of death and desolation. Would that the pen of the historian could record that this aid was followed by a nation's gratitude! But it was not so.'[1] This opinion was echoed by Fletcher and Kipling: 'All British politicians on both sides have, during the last seventy years made haste to remove every real and indeed every imaginary grievance of the Irish people, though they have earned no gratitude by doing so.'[2] A growing mood of irritation with the Irish is expressed by references to their 'great lawlessness'[3] and we even find one, who is otherwise quite sympathetic to them, lamenting the fate of the Irish clergy when the Irish would not pay their tithes: 'The result of this resistance was that many of the clergy were reduced to a state bordering on starvation.'[4] Kipling and Fletcher summed up the Irish character in extreme, if not entirely unrepresentative, terms. They noted that Ireland never had the benefit of being ruled by the Romans and went on: 'so Ireland never went to school and has been a spoilt child ever since, the most charming of children indeed, full of beautiful laughter and tender tears, full of poetry and valour, but incapable of ruling herself and impatient of rule by others.'[5]

As might be expected, the other European nations only make brief appearances in books which deal with English history. Nevertheless, the few references which are made to them are not on the whole uncomplimentary. The Germans, for instance, are recognised to be racially related to the English through their kinship with the Anglo-Saxons so that when Tout described the victories of Marlborough and Prince Eugene, he added that 'the whole teutonic race was represented' in their armies.[6] The French are portrayed as perhaps less trustworthy, but most writers agree in believing them to be brave and intelligent. When describing the work of Edward VII in arranging the *entente cordiale*, the author of the *Tower Readers* described them as 'our bright and witty neighbours'.[7] As we have

---

[1] Farr (1848), p. 461.
[2] Fletcher and Kipling (1911), p. 227.
[3] Ransome (1905), p. 162.
[4] Morris (1882), vol. 4, p. 223.
[5] Fletcher and Kipling (1911), p. 21.
[6] Tout (1890), p. 30.
[7] *Tower* (1911), vol. 7, p. 211.

seen, Napoleon rather than the French people is blamed for the wars of
1793–1815. Fletcher described them as 'brave fellows' before Waterloo[1]
although at another point they are said to be 'cunning' since they
inveigled an unsuspecting Britain into the disastrous Crimean War.[2]

While Europeans were granted some respect, the peoples of Africa and
Asia who came to form part of Britain's Empire were less kindly treated
in the textbooks. It is true that at the beginning of the century Baldwin
was able to express admiration for the temperament and culture of the
Hindoos, 'an innocent race of men, whose only food is rice, and who are
maintained for three half pence a day per man: for them the country is
named Hindoostan: their books on astronomy and other sciences are
extremely ancient: their gods are Brama, Vischnou, and others. . . .'[3]
Later, however, reference was sometimes made to 'the barbaric peoples of
Asia'[4] and the most frequent impression conveyed about the Indians and
their near neighbours, the Afghans, is that they are cruel and totally
unfitted to rule themselves. The Black Hole of Calcutta in which a party of
Englishmen was incarcerated, with the result that most of them died from
suffocation, is widely reported in the textbooks. There abound accounts of
how the victims trampled each other down 'amid the laughter of the
guards'[5] and heard their cries for mercy savagely mocked.[6] In fact eye-
witnesses' accounts from survivors tell us not that the guards laughed, but
that they did their best to bring water to the prisoners. Only one writer
suggested that Surajah Dowlah may not have intended to kill, but merely
to imprison the English. Keightley remarked that he 'does not appear to
have designed their death but it gave him no concern'.[7] Later, the Indian
Mutiny is also treated as yet another example of Oriental cruelty. Several
writers described Nana Sahib as 'a fiend in human shape' or as a 'monster'.[8]
One author commented: 'and truly the barbarous cruelty with which
they had executed this massacre, presented a tale of unheard of horror'.[9]
On the other hand, a significant minority do note the equal brutality of
the English in the suppression of disorder in the Indian sub-continent.

---

[1] Fletcher and Kipling (1911), p. 217.
[2] Ibid. p. 245.
[3] Baldwin (1812), p. 39.
[4] *Cassells' Class History* (1884), p. 378.
[5] Edwards (1901), p. 267.
[6] *Holborn* (1882), Book 2, p. 163.
[7] Keightley (1841), p. 325.
[8] *Jack* (1905), vol. 3, p. 141.
[9] Tegg (1862), p. 86.

There were protests against the suppression of the Indian mutiny: 'Bloody and revolting deeds were committed by them; but they were barbarians while those against whom they were opposed were normal Christians from whom better things might have been expected.'[1] The criticisms were not confined to books for middle-class schools. The author of an elementary school reader wrote: 'So many cruel things had been done, and the hearts of our men were so sore that they committed acts of revenge which, may be, we should now like to forget.'[2] Miss Yonge also stressed the cruelty of the suppression of the mutiny: 'The mutinous Sepoys were hunted down like wild beasts, for revenge had made the British troops very cruel.'[3]

There was also some criticism of British rule in the eighteenth century, though the general opinion in textbooks was that the Indians were lucky to be ruled by the British. The East India Company was criticised for its exploitation of the natives—a typical view being: 'It is much to be lamented that most of the persons employed by the company thought more of enriching themselves than of obeying the dictates of justice and humanity, of sustaining the honour of their country. The natives were pillaged in the most merciless manner.'[4] This view was shared by others who event went so far as to attribute the Indian Mutiny to the corruption of English rule rather than to more widely accepted causes, such as the use of cartridges greased with animal fat which annoyed the Seopys.[5] It is notable that one of the most modest descriptions of English rule in India occurs in a book published there in the years immediately preceeding the mutiny. The author remarked that while admittedly imperfect, English rule was better than those of previous conquerors since it genuinely aimed at the prosperity of the people as a whole.[6]

There is little criticism and much praise for English rule in India after the mutiny, however. The author of the *Pitman's Reader* described how in the time of Lawrence as Viceroy; 'Under his able guidance the natives soon learned to recognise the justice and sound sense of their conquerors and gradually settled down to peaceful work in the rice-fields.'[7] Another writer who portrayed the Indians as sensible enough to recognise that they

---

[1] Farr (1856), p. 456.
[2] *Tower* (1911), vol. 7, p. 161.
[3] Yonge (1890), Book 6, p. 68.
[4] Keightley (1841), p. 325.
[5] Ross (1873), pp. 100–1.
[6] *Introduction to Universal History* (1854), p. 150.
[7] *Pitman* (1901), pp. 190–1.

need firm rule and yet are incapable of providing it for themselves is the author of the *Warwick Readers*. He asserted: 'The people of India see that we desire their welfare and they know it is only our rule which keeps them at peace with one another.'¹ Little praise was given to the fighting qualities of the Indians except when they are under British command when tribute was paid to 'the devotion and gallantry with which the Indian troops obeyed their British officers' during the mutiny.² In contrast even Surajah Dowlah's army was depicted as a 'mob'.³

Much the same condescending and paternalistic attitude was expressed with regard to the African peoples. It is true that they received some sympathy because they were the subjects of the slave trade which is almost universally abhorred. They are the 'poor negroes' of the *Cambridge Readers*.⁴ Nevertheless, it is early in the century that we find the most sympathetic view of the African slave: 'Inhuman acts from which nature recoils in horror inflicted upon men who were guilty of no offence but of inheriting a colour of the skin differing from that of their oppressors or of being a few centuries behind them in civilisation.'⁵ Later writers tend to gloss over or omit details of the slave trade. Nor do they mention colour on the whole. If they do, they assume that the coloured cannot have equal rights with the white races. One author wrote of the Boer War: 'The people within the Queen's dominions were determined that the paramount power in South Africa should be Great Britain, and that the white races south of the Zambesi should have equal rights.'⁶ There is, in Fletcher and Kipling's history, a description of the life of the freed slave in the West Indies which is unique in its severity, though not altogether in its general tone. He was depicted as: 'Lazy, vicious and incapable of serious improvement or of work except under compulsion. In such a climate a few bananas will sustain the life of a negro quite sufficiently; why should he work to get more than this. He is quite happy and quite useless and spends any extra wages which he may earn upon finery.'⁷

These opinions about the native peoples of the Empire are of course closely connected to developing ideas about the need for and justification

---

¹ *Warwick* (1896), vol. 5, p. 200.
² Ibid. vol. 7, p. 230.
³ *Blackwoods* (1883), vol. 3, p. 149.
⁴ *Cambridge* (1911), vol. 1, p. 212.
⁵ Cooper (1830), p. 121.
⁶ Hassall (1901), p. 585.
⁷ Fletcher and Kipling (1911), p. 240.

of imperial rule. The latter was certainly not uniformly admired in the eighteenth century. After the loss of the American colonies the remnants of the Empire were regarded in some circles as a nuisance and expense. However, more favourable views of the nature of imperial power gradually became discernible. Burke, during the War of American Independence, set the keynote for those who believed that imperial rule ought to be beneficial to the people of a colony and that they must be granted full equality with the citizens of the mother country if their loyalty was to be retained. Empire was for him a sacred trust. In a speech of 22 March 1775 he said: 'Magnanimity in politics is not seldom the truest wisdom; and a great empire and little minds go ill together. We ought to elevate our minds to the greatness of that trust to which the order of Providence has called us. By adverting to the dignity of this high calling, our ancestors have turned a savage wilderness into a glorious empire; and have made the most extensive, and the only honourable conquests; not by destroying, but by promoting, the wealth, the number and happiness of the human race.'[1] Throughout the ensuing century as Britain increased its Empire in India and Africa. Burke's ideas remained influential. They were echoed, for instance, by Anthony Trollope, writing in 1872. He claimed that colonies were ruled 'not for our glory, but their happiness' and that when they were given up, 'let us do so with neither smothered jealousy nor with open hostility, but with a proud feeling that we are sending a son out into the world able to take his place among men'.[2] As other less paternalistic attitudes to imperial rule became more popular, voices still continued to be raised on behalf of the subject peoples, insisting that they be treated with respect and humanity. Lingard attacked 'that despotic rule, which takes no account of native customs, traditions and prejudices, is not suited to the successful development of an infant civilization, nor, in my view, is it in accordance with the spirit of English colonial rule.'[3]

It would be naive, however, to take all statements as to the noble paternalism of British imperial rule at their face value. As J. A. Hobson pointed out in 1902, the British were adept at cloaking their political and financial designs with protestations that they were acting for the good of their colonial peoples. This was especially the case in India: 'Although no

---

[1] Quoted in *Documents of English History 1688–1832*, by Barker, St Aubyn and Ollard (1952).
[2] Quoted in *Ideas and Beliefs of the Victorians* (1949), p. 326.
[3] Ibid. p. 412.

candid student of history will maintain for a moment that the entrance of British power into India, and the chief steps leading to the present British Empire there, were motivated by considerations other than our own political and commercial aggrandisement, nothing is more common than to hear the gains which it is alleged the natives of the country have received from British rule assigned as the moral justification of our Indian Empire.'[1] That there is some truth in Hobson's assertions may be seen from Clive's attempt to persuade Pitt and the British Government to interest themselves in India as 'an immense source of wealth to the kingdom'[2] and Gibbon Wakefield's advocacy of settlement in Australia and New Zealand was later also made on the grounds that the mother country would reap financial advantages from the new colonies—an argument designed to soothe the fears of those who had grown disillusioned as to the practical merits of colonisation after the disasters of the War of American Independence.[3] Moreover, it was no accident that in the last part of the nineteenth century when British industry was suffering a recession, partly owing to foreign competition and a shortage of raw materials, British imperial interests were extended to Africa and advocacy of British imperialism was at its height. Even Gladstone had to admit that the new doctrines were popular: 'The dominant passion of England is extended Empire. It has heretofore been kept in check by the integrity and sagacity of her statesmen, who have not shrunk from teaching her the lessons of self-denial and self-restraint. But a new race has arisen and . . . the exercise of moral control over ambition and cupidity, have been left to the intermittent and feeble handling of those who do not govern.'[4] His opponent Disraeli, however, was able to exploit the pro-imperialist tenor of the times. His policy was later supported by such works as Sir John Seeley's *The Expansion of England* which depicted the history of England as a movement towards Empire. The imperialist movement culminated in the Imperial Federation League which was founded after the Jubilee celebrations of 1884 and which had the design of preserving the Empire and welding it still more closely together through a scheme of federal government. Although the League broke up in 1893 after disagreements among its members, im-

---

[1] Quoted in *Documents of English History 1832–1950*, by Barker, St Aubyn and Ollard (1954), p. 76.
[2] Ibid. p. 39.
[3] Ibid. p. 65.
[4] Ibid. p. 73.

perialist ideas continued popular up to the outbreak of the First World
War, although they were under heavy attack.'

Some of the changing opinions about imperial rule are clearly reflected
in history textbooks. Early in the nineteenth century the idea of imposing
English rule on other countries 'for their own good' did not apparently
appeal. Baldwin declared tolerantly that other nations 'love their independence and abhor the idea of becoming a province and an inferior of
another nation: it is the name of ENGLAND that has inspired our soldiers
with bravery and our poets with sublimity and imagination. Scotland is
not less dear to a Scotsman. When a country is no longer its own master,
it loses its peculiar name or that name no longer excites the same glow in
the bosom of the natives.'[1] No doubt Baldwin was well aware how near
England herself had been to being absorbed into Napoleon's Empire
when he wrote these words. Far from regarding the growth of Empire as
desirable, early writers considered it as something of a nuisance, if their
protestations about the loss of the American colonies are to be believed.
One remarked that 'we lost much of our power in America. I believe,
however, we are quite well without it'.[2] and another asserted that they
'had yielded hardly as much as their maintenance cost'.[3]

Such financial considerations go unmentioned by later writers who
almost totally neglect to point out the profitability of Empire and its
connection with the growth of British trade. Instead they tend to regard
Empire as a sacred trust, as well as a matter for pride since 'owing to the
extent of our colonial Empire, the sun never sets upon British dominions'.[4]
The authors of elementary school readers were particularly fond of elabo-
rate variations on this theme. One wrote of 'barbarian peoples whom it is
profitless to conquer, yet amongst whom it is difficult otherwise to en-
force peace and order'.[5] Another gave an idyllic account of the growth and
purpose of the Empire. 'The British Empire at the beginning of the
twentieth century includes lands in every part of the globe, some gained
by the valour of our soldiers, or by the patient toil and steady enterprise
of colonists from the mother country. It embraces people of almost every
race, colour and religion, all living peacefully and prospering under the
British flag, and content with the knowledge that the strong arm and brave

---

[1] Baldwin (1812), p. 59.
[2] Davys (1822), p. 249.
[3] Farr (1848), p. 404.
[4] Littlewood (1869), p. 123.
[5] *Cassells Class History* (1884), p. 400.

spirit that gained freedom for them will always be ready to defend the precious gift.'[1] By the end of the period, therefore, conquest by Britain, far from seeming the degrading business which Baldwin had envisaged was seen to be the beginning and not the end of liberty. It was assumed that all the subject peoples welcomed the peace and order of British rule and that it was the duty rather than the pleasure of the British people to carry out the task of maintaining the Empire. Only the odd solitary voice protested against this. Pitt, the anti-war leader of the Berkeley Mutual Improvement Society of Mitcham in Surrey, spoke out against an empire which must be controlled by force and declared of the other colonies, 'much better to be independent of them, as with Canada and Australia, and trust to goodwill and free trade'.[2]

Yet by the turn of the century it is possible to detect an underlying note of uncertainty about the future of the Empire. Even earlier Milner had recalled the eighteenth-century views of Chapman that all empires must eventually decline. He asserted that our aims should be 'to render England "great among the nations" instead of being added to the history of mighty Empires which have crumbled to dust'.[3] It was perhaps in an effort to suggest that the British Empire was only just beginning rather than declining that some writers begin to stress the need for 'drawing closer the ties existing between mother country and colonies'[4] or for drawing them 'into a world-wide communion by means of the same federal principle'.[5] On the eve of the First World War, which was to be so damaging to English power, Hearnshaw mentioned the idea of imperial federation and remarked: 'England realised "the day of Empire had dawned".'[6] Some of the text-books tend to reflect fears of the time that Britain was the object of a conspiracy of jealous powers whose aim was to ruin her. One author suggested that any sign of weakness would lead to disaster, for he wrote of the Boer War: 'It was absolutely necessary to establish in the mind of the civilised world, and especially of the African world, that any violation of our frontiers would instantly be punished.'[7] Of course it is possible to find instances of a somewhat defensive attitude to Britain'

1 *King Edward Readers* (1901), pp. 5–6.
2 Pitt (1893), p. 99.
3 Milner (1855), p. 803.
4 Hassall (1901), p. 579.
5 Tout (1890), p. 286.
6 Hearnshaw (1914), p. 166.
7 Hassall (1901), p. 585.

role in the world being expressed much earlier in the nineteenth century. For instance, Bishop Davys wrote of William the Conqueror that like all tyrants he was 'greedy for land'. He then went on to add: 'This is generally the case invaders and therefore every man who knows what he is about will do all he can to defend his country from their attacks.'[1] Nevertheless this sort of opinion becomes much more common after 1870 when calls to defend the country began to resound. W. S. Ross praised those who joined the Volunteer movement,[2] and Arabella Buckley stressed the duty of each citizen to see that 'England may not be a declining power as some would have us believe'.[3] The role of the navy is stressed as 'the surest means of defence'[4] or as 'England's bulwark'.[5] Fletcher and Kipling openly stated that there is 'a great deal of jealousy from other European powers',[6] and added: 'The other nations have realised that this Empire was founded on trade, that it has to be maintained by a navy, and that it has resulted in good government of the races subject to us. So, though they have envied us and given us ugly names, they have, on the whole, paid us the compliment of trying to copy us.'[7] This view was also expressed by Hearnshaw, who with unfounded optimism claimed: 'The peace of the continent is maintained chiefly by fear of the appalling consequences of a great modern war.'[8] Hearnshaw's book was published in 1914.

One writer of the period, however, did try to explain the fears of some adults to his readers and to minimise them. The author of the *Tower Reader* explained that while being the possessor of a large empire had its advantages, it also had its dangers. 'We recognise the advantages easily enough, for we see how it opens the whole earth to our enterprise, offers an enormous field to our trade and lays the products of every clime at our feet. . . . But we forget sometimes in our busy money-making moments that such a scattered Empire touches many foreign boundaries and offers numerous points of attack to any enemy. At times, of course, we realise this clearly and acutely and get a little scared. It comes home to us also in such moments that we have 'waxed fat' and that hungrier people, covetous for territory and trade look at us and say "What a glorious time

---

[1] Davys (1822), p. 10.
[2] Ross (1873), p. 76.
[3] Buckley (1904), p. 149.
[4] *Warwick* (1896), vol. 4, p. 120.
[5] *Tower* (1911), vol. 3, p. 161.
[6] Fletcher and Kipling (1911), p. 244.
[7] Ibid. p. 245.
[8] Hearnshaw (1914), p. 174.

we might have if only we could knock John Bull down and rifle his bulging pockets . . .". Perhaps it is only natural that the older he gets and the richer he gets, the more ready he will be to see "bogies".[1] This quotation is particularly significant, not only because it expresses the fears of some Englishmen that others were after their wealth, but also because it reflects an unease that perhaps England has grown too rich at the expense of less fortunate peoples. It is also notable for the moderation with which the author suggests that it is unwise to see threats where in fact none may exist.

It was perhaps this uncertainty about the future of the British Empire which caused authors of textbooks to sharpen their demands for the future loyalty and patriotism of their readers at the turn of the century. A typical view was expressed by Cyril Ransome: 'On us, after all, devolves the responsibility of governing the Empire, and of handing on unimpaired to our descendants the treasures of freedom and dominion which our ancestors acquired and entrusted to us. Nothing is of more vital importance than the carrying out of this trust. It is a duty to which the interests of all parties, of all classes, and all nationalities within the Empire should be subordinate.'[2] A frequent theme in these exhortations is the need to 'prove that we are worthy of those who went before us',[3] by setting a good moral example, or in the words of Charlotte M. Yonge: 'Whoever succeeds in doing his or her duty to God, man and to the country is helping to keep our beloved old England in honour and safety.'[4] Although Miss Yonge suggested to her small readers that they would all know someone who was fighting for Queen and country abroad and who had been decorated for valour—'Sometimes the Queen will put it on with her own hands and thank the man for having done his duty'[5]—she did not openly suggest fighting as a means whereby the pupil could serve his country. Fletcher and Kipling did so in their history. They concluded: 'But I don't think there can be any doubt that the only safe thing for all of us who love our country is to learn soldiering at once and be prepared to fight at any moment.'[6] Most writers, however, avoid this and concentrate on general demands for service and loyal responsibility on the part of the reader.

---

1 *Tower* (1911), vol. 7, pp. 145–6.
2 Ransome (1890), pp. 236–7.
3 Gardiner (1888), p. 221.
4 Yonge (1890), Book 6, p. 75.
5 Ibid. p. 114.
6 Fletcher and Kipling (1911), p. 244.

We have seen that during the years preceding the First World War there is evidence that war was becoming morally acceptable.[1] This, together with the ultra-patriotic tone adopted in many textbooks of the period lends colour to the view that there was an increase in nationalistic propaganda designed to foster a willingness to fight on the part of the rising generation. An examination of opinions about the past wars in which English interests had been involved does not entirely support the 'my country right or wrong' image, however. For instance, accounts of the Hundred Years War show clearly that the textbook writers were able to take a detached attitude with regard to a war of the distant past at least. Baldwin set the tone of comments early in the nineteenth century when he refused to be blinded by the achievements of Henry V's reign and added: 'Those circumstances which constitute its splendour are, in the eyes of reason, its deepest disgrace.'[2] The Hundred Years War is regarded by writers later in the century as an 'unjust war'[3] or as 'not a necessary or at all a wise war',[4] or as 'a folly and a curse'.[5] Moreover, the war is criticised not only because it was immoral in that Edward III's claim to the French throne was 'so unreasonable and so thoroughly disavowed by the French nation, that to insist on it was no better than pretenting to the insolent conquest of the kingdom',[6] but also on the grounds that it was a waste of men and money. The latter in particular comes to be stressed later in the century. The author of the *Jack Readers* noted that English victories were only won 'at the cost of much suffering and misery, and great loss of life and money'.[7] Conan and Kendall are among several writers who suggested that war 'well nigh ruined both nations',[8] and Bullock considered that the wars were 'a fearful waste of blood and treasure' and 'as wicked as anything to be met with in the history of our wars'.[9] It is true, however, that there are a few dissenting voices. One writer described Edward's 'brilliant wars',[10] while another believed that the conquests in France, though they did not last, 'served to elevate the character of the English people, to

---

[1] See above, p. 73-4.
[2] Baldwin (1812), p. 76.
[3] *Cassells* (1884), p. 81.
[4] *Chambers* (1885), p. 76.
[5] Hearnshaw (1914), p. 52.
[6] Hume (1875), p. 175.
[7] *Jack* (1905), vol. 2, p. 156.
[8] Conan and Kendall (1902), p. 114.
[9] Bullock (1861), p. 75.
[10] *Allison* (1840), p. 166.

enlarge their views, and give consistency to their energies'.[1] He was the only one to make a defence of the war on moral grounds, however. A more practical view was that of Symes who credited Edward III with a 'statesmanlike motive' in protecting the wool trade with Flanders from the attacks of the French.[2]

In the description of the course of the wars as opposed to their causes the writers are much less inclined to accept a relatively pro-French point of view. Not unnaturally much space is devoted to describing English victories such as Agincourt, while the equally considerable French success at, for instance, Patay, goes unremarked. One writer claimed of Agincourt: 'Never in the history of the world was so great a victory gained by so small a number over so large an army.'[3] Descriptions such as this one from the *Chambers Reader* are common, especially towards the end of the nineteenth century: 'The English, seeing their king always in the thick of the battle, fought like lions. The French fought bravely too, but it was no use. Before night had come all those who were not killed or made prisoner had run away and left the English flag floating in triumph over the field of Agincourt.'[4] The main features of that passage are that while paying tribute to French courage, the writers suggest that victory for England was inevitable without giving any explanation, e.g. superior weapons or tactics. We are, therefore, left to assume that the English were innately superior as fighters. The last sentence adds a poetic touch to rub in the message that the French 'ran away', leaving England supreme. Moreover, although most writers joined in praising Joan of Arc and considered her trial an 'everlasting disgrace'[5] or 'barbarous conduct',[6] they made sure that it was stressed that the blame for it 'rests with the French as well as the English'.[7] In spite of Joan's success, some writers—a small minority—took the attitude that England should have won the Hundred Years War and was foiled only by the death of Henry V. As Murby put it: 'Had he lived no doubt France would have been completely conquered.'[8]

There is far less evidence of nationalistic feeling in the descriptions of the War of American Independence, another contest in which Britain

---

[1] Gleig (1853), p. 150.
[2] Symes (1899), p. 92.
[3] *Blackwoods* (1883), vol. 2, p. 115.
[4] *Chambers* (1901–5), vol. 3, pp. 50–1.
[5] Murby (1895), p. 56.
[6] *Allison* (1880), p. 220.
[7] Ibid.
[8] Murby (1895), p. 56.

eventually lost a number of her overseas possessions. This may be explained by the fact that there are far fewer English victories of even moderate dimensions to write about in this struggle. As in the Hundred Years War, it is generally admitted that England was fighting an unjust war. It is true that Ross described the Americans as 'malcontents'[1] and that Carter complained that the Americans 'obstinately' refused to pay taxes.[2] Nevertheless, the overwhelming opinion throughout the century agreed that our conduct in America was 'arbitrary and unjust'.[3] Frequently the war was blamed on George III and some of his Ministers: 'But the best and most just of the Ministers said that it was a bad and unjust war and that it would disgrace our country forever.'[4] Even those writers who lived in a time when the war was well within living memory are moderate in their opinions. Baldwin wrote: 'The colonies of America were too large and too distant for us to hope to retain them long in subjection. Yet they had English feeling and spoke the English language.'[5] A generally favourable attitude was also adopted towards the colonists' leader in the war, George Washington. There are descriptions of his 'noble patience'[6] and how 'he was venerated by his own countrymen and cannot but be respected by ours'.[7]

The course of the war is, not surprisingly, seen by most writers as an unmitigated disaster for Britain. Gleig expressed a typical view: 'Thus ended the most disastrous war in which Great Britain was ever engaged which, as it had been entered into at the beginning rashly, heedlessly, wantonly, so it was carried out at least in the colonies without either skill or judgment to the last.'[8] It is true that a significant group of writers held 'the success of the Americans in securing their independence was due principally to the French alliance without which it is hard to see how the colonists could have succeeded',[9] and the author of *Warwick Readers* perhaps echoing the more bellicose mood at the end of the century, declared: 'Hardly ever had any country to fight so many enemies at once and come out of the struggle so creditably.'[10] Nevertheless, the general

---

[1] Ross (1873), p. 96.
[2] Carter (1900), p. 105.
[3] Bullock (1861), p. 212.
[4] *Granville* (1885), p. 153.
[5] Baldwin (1812), p. 138.
[6] *Royal Series* (1874), p. 137.
[7] Birkby (1869), p. 163.
[8] Gleig (1861), p. 519.
[9] Hassall (1901), p. 486.
[10] *Warwick*, vol. 5, p. 163.

view throughout the nineteenth century is that the war was a 'miserable contest'[1] and that by it 'England received a lesson which she well deserved'.[2] The *Jack Reader* adds: 'We cannot but look back upon this page of our history with feelings of shame and regret.'[3]

It may be that the comparatively moderate and self-critical views expressed about the Hundred Years War and the War of American Independence stem from the fact that they were wars of the past which England had lost. The Napoleonic Wars, being more recent in time and resulting in a victory for England and her allies, might be expected to show more evidence of extreme nationalistic bias. Such is not, on the whole, the case. It is strange to find Baldwin at the beginning of the century conceding that at the peace of Amiens 'France was finally victorious', and hailing Napoleon as a 'very extraordinary man'.[4] Much the same words were used by Hort, another early writer.[5] It is possible to tell that these were not exceptional views of one who was England's greatest enemy in his day. Mrs Helme's history was severely criticised in the *Quarterly Journal of Education* on the grounds that the writer was 'so vituperative against Napoleon' that the reviewer suggested that she had 'borrowed a page from "Cursing made easy" by Dr Slop'.[6] Later in the century views about Napoleon are evenly divided. Those who admire his stress 'his greatness',[7] his 'military genius'[8] or his 'victorious career'.[9] With apparent impartiality Cooper hailed him with Wellington as 'the two greatest commanders of the age.[10] On the other hand Napoleon is also portrayed as guilty of 'restless projects of unprincipled ambition',[11] as 'despotic and theatrical',[12] 'proud'[13] and as always thinking of himself and his own glory in contrast to Nelson who merely tried to do his duty to England.[14] Many writers see in him a threat to life and liberty for the peoples of Europe whom he afflicted with his ambitious designs. A typical view was expressed by the author of the

---

[1] Hort (1822), p. 202.
[2] Gardiner (1888), p. 519.
[3] *Jack* (1905), vol. 3, p. 71.
[4] Baldwin (1812), p. 141.
[5] Hort (1822), p. 205.
[6] July—October 1831, p. 367.
[7] Bullock (1861), p. 234.
[8] *Chambers* (1885), p. 188.
[9] *Collins* (1890), p. 201.
[10] Cooper (1843), p. 156.
[11] Birkby (1869), p. 184.
[12] Bright (1875), p. 1347.
[13] *Cassells' Simple Outline* (1884), p. 168.
[14] Ibid.

Jack Readers. He wrote of the importance of Napoleon's career 'which was to be of such fearful moment to the human race whose lives and liberties this scourge of Europe held so cheap'.[1] It is possibly true that opinions about Napoleon hardened towards the end of the nineteenth century, but on the whole views which did not regard him with too much disfavour continued to be expressed.

When we come to consider the comments on the course of the war we find that, as we might expect, much space is expended on the careers of Nelson and Wellington and the French defeat is attributed largely to their skill and the courage of the men under their command. Thus Ransome summed up the latter's career: 'Nelson's victory made England mistress of the seas and we had nothing more to fear from our enemies' fleets.'[2] Likewise Wellington's victory at Waterloo is said to have resulted in Napoleon fleeing the field 'where his mighty sword, stained with the blood of millions, lay shivered in atoms'.[3] On the whole little credit is given to England's allies for the victory. In most books Blucher is scarcely mentioned more than in this brief reference to his presence at Waterloo in the Mnemonic history of England: 'Bonaparte from Blücher and Welling-ton retreated',[4] and even here we may feel that he gets unusual prominence because his name happens to begin with a letter which fits in with the author's scheme. Kipling even went so far as to deny Blücher's importance in the battle: 'But at last he came, though his men did not get into action till about 4.30 p.m. and did not produce much effect on the French for two hours more.'[5] Only one writer appears to have remarked on the fact that it was Napoleon's defeat in Russia which really ended his power, and he, not surprisingly, was a contemporary of events. Cooper declared: 'In the smoke of Moscow the prosperity of Bonaparte evaporated.'[6]

The Opium Wars against China provide us with a comparison between the moderate attitude of writers at the beginning of the century towards events of their own time and the much more nationalistic approach later in the century. The majority of opinion appears to be that Britain was fully justified in her actions against an awkward and recalcitrant people who refused to accept the benefits of European commerce, and despised

---

[1] *Jack* (1905), vol. 3, p. 84.
[2] Ransome (1905), p. 361.
[3] *Royal Schools* (1875), p. 45.
[4] Matthews (1830), p. 9.
[5] Fletcher and Kipling (1911), p. 217.
[6] Cooper (1830), p. 167.

Western culture. Several writers stressed that the Chinese regarded the English as 'barbarians',[1] or suggested that the only reason the Chinese opposed the import of opium in the first place was from their fear that English merchants were competing with their own trade in the drug,[2] and that Chinese opium ships came and went as usual after the ban on the opium trade.[3] The author of the *Royal School Series*, far from stressing the harmful nature of the drug, merely remarked that the Chinese love to smoke it, implying that their government was merely denying them an innocent pleasure by preventing its importation.[4] Miss Rodwell did not mention opium at all, but attributed the first war to 'some unfair dealings on the part of the Chinese. . . . The Chinese are a very cold kind of people and do not like strangers to go among them'.[5] The second war which broke out when the Chinese fired on the *Arrow*, a ship bearing, but not entitled to fly, the British flag, is similarly attributed to the action of the Chinese. Hostilities are said to have begun in consequence of 'the arrogance of Chinese Commissioner Yeh'[6] and the 'insult to the British flag'.[7] One writer recorded with apparent satisfaction that the war 'fought in alliance with the French to avenge the treachery of the Chinese government was brought to a triumphant issue by the entry of our troops into Pekin and the sacking of the summer palace'.[8] Palmerston is repeatedly praised for his actions with regard to China. He was described as 'a typical Englishman. Englishmen have a love of freedom and they delight in the consciousness of power. Lord Palmerston protected the struggling little nations and, so doing, he snubbed the big ones . . . his policy of boisterous diplomacy united righteousness and profit.'[9]

However, there remain a substantial number of writers who were uneasy or downright hostile to Palmerston's policy on moral grounds. One expressed his unease by saying: 'The injustice of the war was strongly felt by the British nation: but it was hoped that by it a door might be opened for preaching the Gospel in that vast Empire, an Empire certainly more than 300 million human beings all bowing down to gods of wood and

---

[1] Birkby (1869), p. 210.
[2] Corner (1885), pp. 312–3.
[3] Maunder (1864), p. 501.
[4] *Royal School Series* (1874), p. 180.
[5] Rodwell (1853), p. 244.
[6] Murby (1895), p. 168.
[7] Pringle (1871), p. 135.
[8] *Cassells Class History* (1884), p. 392.
[9] Edwards (1901), p. 324.

stone.'[1] His arguments were attacked by several writers, however. Curtis dismissed them and added: 'We must not disguise the fact that the war was undertaken on pretexts that were largely, if not entirely, unjustifiable.'[2] McCarthy tried to destroy the argument that the Chinese were ignorant savages: 'They had laws, literature, faiths, morals, and a system of government',[3] while Pitt denies that there could be any excuse for a Christian to uphold the wars. 'It helped our interests, of course, but that plea will hardly stand at the Day of Judgment. And then we have the conceited impudence to send missionaries to teach them religion!'[4] Other writers declared that the war was 'important in the history of the opening of China to Western civilization through British efforts and illustrates the worst aspects of our policy to weaker states',[5] or merely stated: 'We were completely in the wrong.' There was, therefore, a substantial body of opinion among textbook writers which judged government policy even of recent date on moral rather than nationalistic grounds, and more important, was not afraid to say so. McCarthy in fact even dared to hint that some of those who defend the war had financial interests at stake: 'As human nature is constituted it becomes very easy for most of us to find excuses for the traffic out of which our uncles are to become wealthy and of whom we are to be in great part the heir.'[6] It is interesting that McCarthy's book, which must strike the modern reader as far more liberal in tone than most others of the period, was favourably reviewed in at least one publication on its appearance.[7]

Nevertheless it is certainly true that history textbooks became more jingoistic towards the end of the nineteenth century. The stress on the grandeur of British dominions and the ideal of empire, descriptions of a noble national stereotype compared to inferior races, homilies on the need for patriotic duty—all these suggest an intensification of national feeling. Whether this feeling played a part in bringing war nearer or was itself mainly the product of tension in Europe is a matter for conjecture. It is none the less remarkable that at such a time so many authors of children's textbooks succeeded in maintaining a critical attitude to the conduct of

---

[1] Farr (1848), p. 455.
[2] Curtis (1880), p. 500.
[3] McCarthy, *England after the Reform Bill* (1899), p. 154.
[4] Pitt (1893), p. 95.
[5] Rolleston (1902), p. 282.
[6] McCarthy, *England after the Reform Bill* (1899), pp. 158-9.
[7] *Educational Review* (Aug. 1899), pp. 538-9.

their own nation abroad. The tradition that power entailed moral duties stood firm against the claims of a 'my country right or wrong' attitude. Even when actions were justified on grounds which might seem suspect, the mere fact that such a justification was deemed to be necessary must necessarily have encouraged considerable discussion about international matters. If there were those who sought to encourage the unthinking obedience to the call of patriotism which goes to produce 'cannon fodder', they were only rarely to be found among the writers of history textbooks.

History as Tradition

'If they wished to have anything to do with the shaping of this great country in the future, nothing would help them to perform that duty better than trying to find out how we became a great country and what were our traditions.'[1]

THE certainty and simplicity of many opinions expressed in history textbooks of the past is one of their most striking features. It is this which renders them liable to the ridicule of a more cynical age. The fact that opinions were expressed in such forthright terms, and not merely in books designed for the younger age group for whom simplification of expression was necessary, lends colour to the idea that authors were writing with a propagandist aim. Yet much of this is a mere surface impression stemming from our sophistication and wariness about asserting anything which might imply a dogmatic belief in moral and religious absolutes in an age when these are so contested. Judged by the general standards of debate in Victorian England, the opinions expressed in books designed for children do not bear the marks of extremism which may be one of the hallmarks of propaganda. It is perhaps rather in the nature of education in society and the study of history as a part of this that we may see how the forces of conservatism and conformity were, perhaps necessarily, over-represented.

Certainly there do appear to have been certain obvious elements in the opinions expressed in all types of history textbooks which lend colour to the view that they were designed to educate the rising generations to uphold the tradition of society rather than to reform it. The myths of class were gradually changed during the nineteenth century to uphold the new *status quo*. When power had partly passed to the upper middle classes, their standards were held as the ideal and only towards the end of the period were expressions of disapproval and contempt for the lower classes even

---

[1] Report of a speech by W. E. Forster at the prize giving of the Lancashire and Cheshire Institutes (Nov. 1871, p. 237).

[139]

modified. Certainly notions of social equality were conspicuous by their absence. In fact there was a complacency of tone about the condition of society and of the constitution which militated against the pupil being encouraged to consider change in the future. The radicals' doctrine of progress was turned against them. In the same way descriptions of their activities were used to discredit the Chartists, for instance, although many of their demands actually had become law by the time their critics were writing. In addition, notions of morality which fitted in with the dictates of political economy by stressing avoidance of waste and sexual misconduct added to the 'preaching' tone of many textbooks. Even a convenient scapegoat at home for the shortcomings of the past was provided by the Roman Catholic minority. Abroad the villain was any nation who coveted England's Empire, and calls for loyalty and patriotic action were justified by reference to their threats. At the centre of the England created by the textbook writers stood the monarchy and personal descriptions of the actions and qualities of the reigning sovereign abounded, being often associated with the call to 'duty', especially in those works intended for use in the elementary schools.

There is another side to the picture, however. Many of these views appear to have been a natural reflection of the social background and outlook of the authors of textbooks. Moreover, anti-radical opinions became less and not more extreme after the 1870 Education Act when the process of 'educating their masters' was intensified, as one might expect. Nor do all opinions fit in with the idea that the aim of writers was to foster a noncritical attitude to events in their young readers. The saving grace of the Victorian history textbook, viewed in this light, was its emphasis on moral rectitude, supported by the sanctions of religion. Thus the monarchy might be sacrosanct, but individual monarchs were judged in moral terms and their actions subjected to the fiercest scrutiny. Warfare might be necessary, but for many writers it was still evil and its exponents to be abhorred or pitied according to circumstances. Even the nationalism of the turn of the century was tempered by the need to justify action on moral grounds. The power which England enjoyed over 'less fortunate' races was considered both a proof of righteousness or of divine approval, and dependent on it. The concern with morality was by no means confined to the imagination of the textbook writers. It actually existed as a force in society and was exploited politically by Gladstone among others. Springing as it did from the evangelical movement, it was not a comfortable or conformist force for it placed emphasis on individual judgment about the concerns of the nation and set standards above mere convenience by which statesmen of the past and present should be judged. These standards underly many of the opinions which are to be found in history textbooks.

Nevertheless, although they may be acquitted of being purveyors of monolithic propaganda for the ruling classes, textbook writers were perhaps in a more subtle way a brake on changing opinion. Many of the views expressed in textbooks are reflections of those widely held in society at the time when they were written. Thus the fears of revolution and the advance of democracy which resulted from radical and Chartist disturbances are clearly mirrored in savage attacks on political change in the middle years of the nineteenth century. The growing nationalism of the later years was almost at once reflected in the stress on national greatness and the glories of imperialism. However, books were in use long after their first appearance. A popular book, such as the histories of Mrs Markham and Charlotte Yonge, might be in use and widely read for many decades. In the first half of the nineteenth century books were in use which reflected the rationalist and latitudinarian ideas of the eighteenth-century enlightenment, by then submerged by the forces of romanticism and evangelical fervour. In this way the young were subjected to the opinions of their grandfathers as well as their fathers. Certainly such a state of affairs would not be likely to lead to a gathering momentum of ideas in society or even, at a lower level, to adventurous discussion in the classroom.

In addition history was and is a study in which tradition must by definition be stressed. Nor is this necessarily harmful. The traditions of civil and religious liberty, and of the obligations of citizenship, for instance, were noble ones, and the mention of them in history textbooks perhaps necessary and beneficial in its results to the stability of society. It is unfortunate that new and potentially disruptive ideas were omitted, however. Very often these were precisely those on which discussion in the society in which the pupils were to grow up most concentrated and where most uncertainty was felt. It is of course not surprising that there was no mention of republicanism at a time when the future of the monarchy was most in doubt, of atheism or agnosticism, when scientific discovery had apparently undermined fundamentalist belief in the Scriptures, of the rights of women when the battle for these was well under way. No doubt writers were not anxious to disturb themselves or their publishers or readers with such controversies. Nor were they likely to blight the optimism of youth by mounting a full-scale attack on the idea of the inevitable progress of society even though there loomed ahead a war which crippled the civilization of

Western Europe and cost the lives of many of the children who studied their books. These omissions are understandable, but they do throw doubt on the argument used for the study of history, namely, that by study of the institutions and ideas of the past, the young citizen is necessarily prepared to judge the issues of the future. On the contrary, these were the very points at which a voluntary censorship operated on the part of the writers of history books, thereby throwing greater onus on the hard-pressed teacher to remedy the deficiency.

This argument might well apply with equal force to history teaching in our own day. Indeed, there is no excuse for the amusement which often greets some of the more extreme opinions of Victorian England as expressed in children's books. They were often saved from being agents of complacency by the willingness of authors to risk an opinion or to make a judgment on some controversial aspect of the past. They were sustained in this by certainties about the moral, religious and political order which in our more cautious and agnostic age we lack. Nevertheless it may be doubted that the modern penchant for facts—interestingly reported or programmed as they may be—without judgments is not more truly redolent of complacency and of an unwillingness to face the implications of human actions. Victorian textbooks were full of the horror of the death of a few hundred protestant martyrs of Mary's reign; their modern counterparts describe the suffering of millions in concentration or forced labour camps or in bombing raids without undue emphasis. History as a study can impart the opiate of tradition to the rising generation. With a critical spirit it can be a stimulant to constructive change.

BIBLIOGRAPHY

History Textbooks[1]

ADAMS, W. B. *Leading Events in English History* (1872). J

AIRY, O. Textbook of English History from the earliest times (1898). S

ALLISON'S Guide to English History and Bibliography by the Rev. Dr. Brewer (c.1880) 56th ed. J*

AVON Historical Reader (Pitman), Vols. 1 and 3 (1895). J

BALDWIN, E. History of England for the use of Schools and young persons (1812) and (1854). J*

BARTLE, G. A Synopsis of English History (1865). S

BARTLETT's Historical Examiner (1871). S

BEALE, D. The Student's textbook of English and General History (1858). S

BEARD, J. The Scholar's Summary (1875). S

BERKELEY, E. Great Events of English History (1873). J

BIRCHALL's England under the Revolution and the House of Hanover (1876). S

BIRKBY, T. S. History of England from the Roman period to the present time (1869) S

BLACKWOODS Educational Series (edited Meiklejohn), Vols. 1–3 (1883). J

BOURNE, J. E. Granny's History of England (c.1870). J

BOWES, A. A Practical Synopsis of English History (1863) S

BRIEF memoirs of the Leading Events of English History (1806). S

BREWER, Dr. (See Allison's guide).

BRIGHT, J. F. English History for the use of Public Schools (1875). S*

BRITISH History for the Use of Schools and Families (1846). J

BUCKLEY, A. The History of England for Beginners (1904). J

BULLOCK, T. and F. The illustrated History of England (1861). J

CALLCOTT, Lady. Little Arthur's History of England (1962) and (1872); (1st edition 1834). J*

CAMBRIDGE History Readers (1911). J

CARTER, G. History of England in Three Parts (c.1900). S

CATHOLIC Child's History of England (1890). J

CASSELLS Readers for Elementary Schools (1883). J*

CASSELLS Class History of England (1884). J

CASSELLS Simple Outline of English History (1884). J

CASSELLS Simple Stories from English History (1884). J

CATECHISM of English History by a Friend to Youth (1810). J

---

[1] Textbooks are arranged alphabetically under the names of authors. Where the author is unknown the book appears under its title. J = more suited to Junior pupils under thirteen years of age; S = more suited to Senior pupils.
* Denotes that the book had a wide sale or influence.

CHAMBERS Senior English History for Standards V and VI (1885).   J

CHAMBERS New Scheme History Readers (1901–5), 6 Vols.   J*

CHEPMELLS Short Course of History (1849 and 1851).   S

CHESTERFIELD, 5th Earl of. (Philip Henry Stanhope). History of England (1836–53).   S

CLINTON, H. R. A Compendium of English History (1874).   S

CLOUGH, C. History of England for the Young (*c*.1870).   S

COBBETT, W. A History of the Protestant Reformation in England and Ireland (1824).   S

COCKRAN'S Concise History of England (1859).   S

COLLIER, W. F. History of the Nineteenth Century for Schools (1869).   S

COLLIER, W. F. History of England for Junior Classes (1870).   J*

COLLIER, W. F. History of the British Empire (1875).   S

COLLINS Advanced Historical Reader (1890).   J

CONAN, K. and KENDALL, E. A Short History of England for Schools (1902).   S

COOPER'S History of England (on a plan of the Earl of Chesterfield) (1830 and 1843).   S

CORKRAN, J. F. Concise History of England (1859).   S

CORNER, J. History of England (1885). 55th Thousand.   J

CURTIS, J. C. A School and College History of England (1860).   S*

CURTIS, J. C. Elements of the History of England (1875).   S

CURTIS, J. C. Outlines of English History (1891).   S

DARTON'S New History of England (1812).   J

DAVYS, G. A. Plain and Short History of England for Children (1822).   J*

DICKENS, C. Child's History of England (1922 ed.).   J

DODSLEY, R. The Chronicle of the Kings of England (1796), and (1799).   S

DRANE, A. T. History of England for Family use and Upper Classes of Schools.   S

DYMOCK'S abridgement of Goldsmith's History of England (*c*.1870).   S

EASTWOOD, C. H. Student's Synopsis of English History (based on Oman) (1871).   S

EASY History for Upper Standards (c.1885).   J

EDWARDS, O. M. E. A School History of England (1901).   S

ELSON, H. Classified Facts of English History (1872).   S

ENGLISH History for Children (1845).   S

ENGLISH History made Easy (1828).   S

FARR'S School, Collegiate and Family History (1856).   S

FEARENSIDE, C. S. Matriculation Modern History (1902).   S

FLANAGAN, T. A Short Catechism of English History (c.1850).   J

FLETCHER, C. R. L. and KIPLING, R. A School History of England (1911).   J

GARDINER, S. R. New Historical Reader (1888).   J*

GARDINER, S. R. A Student's History of England (1891).   S

GILL'S History of England in lessons for home use (1870).   J

GLEIG'S School History of England to 1837 (1853, 4th ed.).   J*

GRANVILLE History Readers (by T. J. Livesey) (1885 and 1902 eds.).   J

GRIMALDI, S. The Synopsis of English History (1871).   S

HACK, (Mrs.) Stories from English History (revised ed. 1872); (first ed. c. 1820).

HAMILTON, W. Douglas Outlines of English History (1853). S

HASSALL, A. A Class-book of English History (1901). S

HEARNSHAW, F. C. J. The first Book of English History (1914). J

HISTORICAL Reason Why (1859). S

HISTORY of England Mostly in Words of One Syllable (c.1907). J

HISTORY of England from the invasion of Julius Caesar to the Reign of George IV (1825). S

HOLBORN Historical Series (1882). J

HORT, W. J. Epitome of the History of England (1822). S

HUME. The Students' (1875). S*

INCE and GILBERT Outline of English History (1859). S*

INTRODUCTION to universal history for the use of Schools (1854; 1st ed. 1831). J

JACK Historical Readers (1904). J

KIPLING, R. (see Fletcher).

KEIGHTLEY, T. Elementary History of England (1841). S

KNIGHT's School History of England (1865). S

LAURIE, J. S. English History Simplified (1866). J

LAURIE, J. S. Henry's First History of England (1868). J

LEGGE's Reading Book of English History (1864). J

LEGGE's Handy Book of English History (1873). S

LINGARD, J. History of England (continued by N. Birt), (c.1870). S

LITTLEWOOD, W. E. Elementary History of England (1869). J

LITTLEWOOD, W. E. Essentials of English History (1865). S

LIVESEY, T. J. Primer of English History (1877). J

LIVESEY, T. J. English History Readers (1881). J

LIVESEY, T. J. Granville History Readers (1885 and 1902). J

LIVESEY, T. J. and BENSONTHORP History of England (1908). S

MCCARTHY, J. England Before and After the Reform Bill (1899). (Two Vols.) S

MACDOUGALL's School History of Great Britain and Ireland (1904). S

MAGNALLS Historical and Miscellaneous Questions (1800). J*

MAHON, Lord see Chesterfield, Earl of)

MARKHAM, (Mrs.) (Elizabeth Penrose) History of England (1874; 1st ed. 1823). J*

MATHEWS, W. F. Mnemonic texts of English History (1830). J

MAUNDER, S. Treasury of History (1864). S

MILNER, T. History of England (c.1854). S

MORE Stories selected from the History of England (1821). J

MORISON's Time-table of English History (1901). S

MORRIS, D. A Class-book of English History (1871). S*

MORRIS, D. Historical Readers (1822) (4 Vols.).

MORRIS, D. Senior Standard Readers (1883) (3 Vols.). J

MURBY, T. Analysis of English History (1895, 92nd ed.).

NICHOLS, C. H. S. Outlines of English History (1850). S

NISBET's English History (1832). J

OMAN, C. and M. Junior History of England   J

OMAN, C. (see Eastwood)

OXFORD History Readers (1916).   J

PEMBRIDGE, J. A Chronological Table of the Principal events of English History (1868).   S

PICTURES from English History (1846).   J

PINNOCK's Catechism of English History (1822).   S

PITMAN's King Edward History Readers (1901).   J

PITT, G. History of England with the Wars left out (1893, 3rd ed.).   S

PRINGLE, R. S. Local Examination History (1907).   S

QUESTIONS and Answers on the Reigns of the Four Georges, by M.P.H. (1835).   J

RALEIGH History Handbooks, Vol. V. (1897).   J

RANSOME, C. Elementary History for Schools (1890).   J

RANSOME, C. Advanced History (1895).   S

RANSOME, C. (Mrs.) First History of England (1903).   J

RANSOME, C. (Mrs.) Primary History of England (1905).   J

RODWELL, A. Child's first steps to English History (1853; 1st ed. 1844).   J

ROLLESTON, M. A. An English History Note-book (1902).   S

ROSS, W. S. Last Century of British History (1870).   S

ROSS, W. S. A Comprehensive History of England (1872).   S

ROSS, W. S. English History (1873).   S

ROWLEY, J. English History Methodized (1872).   S

ROWLEY, J. Rise of the People (1876).   J

ROYAL School History of Great Britain (1874).   J

ROYAL School Intermediate History of England (1884).   J

ROYAL English History Readers (c.1880).   J

ROYAL Purse Books: Pictures and Stories from English History (1891).   J

SCOTT and FARR History of England (1861).   S

SCHMITZ, L. History of England for Junior Classes (1873).   J

SELBY, C. Events to be remembered in the History of England (1852).   S

SEWELL, E. M. and YONGE, C. M. Historical Selections (1868).   J

SEWELL, E. M. A Catechism of English History (1872).   J

SEYMOUR's Elementary Series No. 1 (1880).   J

STEPPING Stones to English History (1862).   J

SYMES, E. S. English History (1899).   S

TAIT, C. W. A. Analysis of English History (1878).   S

TAYLOR, Emily Stories from History (c.1850).   J.

TEGG's First Book of English History (by Miss Edmunds) (1862)   J

THOMSON, E. England (1885).   S

TOUT, T. F. and YORK POWELL History of England (1890, Part III; 1903, Part II).   S

TOUT, T. F. A Short Analysis of English History (1891).   J

TOWER History Readers (Pitman) (1911).   J

TRIMMER, (Mrs.) History of England (1849).   J

TYTLER, and NARES, O. History of England (c.1860).   S

WHITE, J. History of England to 1848 (1860).   S

WARWICK History Readers (1895–6), 7 Vols.   J

YARNOLD, J. R. Handbook of Lessons in English History (*c.*1870). J
YATES, M. T. Standard History of England (*c.*1872). S
YONGE, C. M. English History Reading Books 1–6 (1880). J*
YONGE, C. M. Simple stories (1890). J
YONGE, C. M. Westminster Reading Books 1–6 (1890). J*

Periodicals 1800–1914
Education: the monthly paper of the National Society 1872–5.
Education: a journal 1890.
Educator, The, 1851–4.
Educational Calendar and Scholastic Year-book 1867–72.
Educational Expositor 1853–5.
Educational Gazette 1855–7.
Educational Guardian 1860–3.
Educational Magazine 1835–6; 1839–41.
Educational Record 1848.
Educational Reporter 1869.
Educational Review 1871, 1891–1901, 1913–4.
Educatioanl Review and Magazine 1826–7.
Educational Times 1853–1914.
Educational Year-book 1879–1885.
Guardian of Education 1802–06.
National Schoolmaster 1871–78.
Pupil Teacher 1876–80.
Quarterly Journal of Education 1831–35; 1872–75.
School Board Chronicle 1871–75.
Schoolmaster's Calendar 1903.
Transactions of the Education Society 1884–85.

Books, Pamphlets and Articles on Education 1800–1914
ADKINS, F. J. Significant History. History (1912).
BARROW, W. Essay on Education (1802).
BECK, A. A. Loose Hints on Education (1781).
BOARD of Education Circular No. 399: The Teaching of History (1908).
BROWNING, P. Oscar, Address to Royal Historical Society (1887).
CHAPMAN, G. A Treatise on Education (1790).
CHAPONE, (Mrs.) Letters on the Improvement of Mind (1820).
CHESTERFIELD, 4th Earl of Letters from a Nobleman to his Son (1810 ed.).
DEBATE on the Education Bill of 1870.
EDGEWORTH, M. Professional Education (1808).
FITCH, J. G. Lectures on Teaching (1885).
FLORIAN, J. B. An essay on an Analytical Course of Studies (c.1780).
FORTY-FOUR Years of the Education Question (1914).
GOOCH, C. P. History and Historians in the Nineteenth Century (1913).
HEADLAM, J. The Effect of the War on the Teaching of History. History (1918).
HEARNSHAW, F. C. J. Place of History in Education. History (1912).

HISTORY Teaching in Education. History (1912).
JOHNSTONE, H. Seven Deadly Sins of History Teaching (1912).
KEATINGE, M. W. Studies in the Teaching of History (1910).
L.C.C. Report on the Teaching of History (1911).
LUCAS, C. P. On the Teaching of Imperial History. History New Series 1 (1916).
MARTEN, C. H. K. Some General Reflections. History (1913).
MORE, H. Hints on the Education of a Young Princess (1805).
NEW CODE for Day Schools (1900–1).
NICHOLSON, G. On Education (1812).
NITHESAY Miscellany or Selections and Extracts on Education (1812).
OWEN, R. System of Education in New Lanark (1824).
PRIESTLEY, J. Miscellaneous Observations Concerning Education (1812 ed.).
PUBLIC Pearl, The, (1854).
ST. JOHN, J. A. Education of the People (1858).
SARGANT, W. L. Essays of a Birmingham Manufacturer (1870).
SCHOOL and the World (1872).
SHEPHERD, Joyce and CARPENTER, Systematic Education (1815).
SIMPSON, J. The Philosophy of Education (1836).
SMITH, W. Student's Vade Mecum (1770).
SPENCER, H. Essays on Education (1911 ed.).
TEACHING of History in Secular Schools (1908). See also Board of Education.
THRING, E. Education and School (1864).
WATSON, Foster. Beginning of the Teaching of Modern Subjects (1909).
WEBB, W. H. History, Patriotism and the Child. History (1913).
WHEELER, F. T. B. What History does for the Boy. History New Series 3 (1918).
WHITMINSTER Secular School Inauguration (1884).

Other Works 1800–1914

CARLYLE, T. Past and Present.
COLERIDGE, C. C. M. Yonge: Her Life and Letters (1903).
DICEY, A. V. Law and Opinion in England (1905).
FARR's Pilgrim Battles: Cross and Crescent (n.d.).
FLAWS, G. C. Sketch of the Life of Saladin (1885).
HITHERSAY, R. B. and ERNEST, G. Sketch of the Life of Saladin (1887).
MACAULAY Essays (1901 ed.).
ROMANES, E. C. M. Yonge (1908).
STRAUSS, R. Robert Dodsley (1910).
SCHMITZ, L. Testimonials in favour of a candidate for the Rectorship of the High School, Edinburgh (n.d.).
SEWELL, E. M. Autobiography (1907).

Other Secondary Works

BARKER, ST. AUBYN and OLLARD. Documents of English History 1688–1832 (1952) and 1832–1950 (1954).
COBBETT, W. Opinions of William Cobbett edited by G. D. H. and M. Cole (1941).

[148]

DANCE, E. H. The Teaching of History (UNESCO, 1955).

DANCE, E. H. History the Betrayer (1960).

ENSOR, R. C. K. England 1870–1914 (1936).

EVANS, J. (ed.). The Victorians (1966).

HANS, N. New Trends in Education in the Eighteenth Century (1951).

HOWAT, G. M. D. The Nineteenth Century History Text-book (British Journal of Educational Studies, May, 1965).

IDEAS and Beliefs of the Victorians (Sylvan Press, 1949).

JULL, E. S. School History Text-books and the Commonwealth (Educational Review, June, 1962).

KNOWLES, C. H. Simon de Montfort (Historical Association, 1965).

KUNITZ and HAYCRAFT British Authors of the Nineteenth Century (1936).

LAUWERYS, J. A. History Text-books and International Understanding (1951).

MCKISACK, M. Edward III and the Historians (History, 1960).

MARTEN, C. H. K. The History of History Teaching (1938).

MARTIN, K. The Crown and the Establishment (1962).

ROBSON, R. (Ed.) Ideas and Institutions of Victoria Britain (1967).

SIMON, B. Studies in the History of Education 1789–1870 and 1870–1914 (1960).

WILLEY, B. The Eighteenth Century Background (1953) and Nineteenth Century Studies (1949).

WILLIAMS, R. Culture and Society 1780–1950 (1958).

WOODWARD, E. L. The Age of Reform (1938).

INDEX